D1531971

Effective Supervision

A Task-Oriented Model for the Mental Health Professions

Effective Supervision

A Task-Oriented Model for the Mental Health Professions

D. Eugene Mead, Ed.D.

BRUNNER/MAZEL, *Publishers* • New York

Library of Congress Cataloging-in-Publication Data
Mead, D. Eugene (Donald Eugene)
  Effective supervision : a task-oriented model for the mental
health professions / D. Eugene Mead
    p.   cm.
  Includes bibliographical references (p.   ) and indexes.
  ISBN 0-87630-600-8
  1. Psychotherapy—Study and teaching—Supervision.   I. Title.
RC459.M43   1990
616.89'14—dc20   90-2257
                                                          CIP

Newbridge Book Clubs
For information about our audio products, write us at:
Newbridge Book Clubs, 3000 Cindel Drive, Delran, NJ 08370

Published by
BRUNNER/MAZEL, INC.
19 Union Square West
New York, New York 10003

Manufactured in the United States of America
10 9 8 7 6 5 4 3 2 1

Contents

Illustrations

Preface

This text is designed to provide professionals in the mental health fields with the opportunity to become acquainted with the research and theory related to supervision. In addition, it provides a general procedural model of the tasks required of supervisors regardless of their preferred theory of therapy. The Task-Oriented Model has several purposes. It serves to structure the tasks required of a supervisor in managing the critical issues related to supervision; it serves as a basis for discussion of the three systems encountered in supervision—the clients' system, the system of the therapist interacting with the clients, and the supervisor-therapist-client system. Finally, the Task-Oriented Model could form the foundation from which to build one's own personal model of supervision and begin the lifelong process of becoming a supervisor.

Acknowledgments

I would like to thank the Brigham Young University Department of Independent Studies for permission to use material from the Independent Study Course Family Sciences 750, Supervision in Marriage and Family Therapy.

Special appreciation to Annette Hoxie who has contributed greatly to the word processing of the typescript and especially to the figures used in this text. Thank you to Robert H. Dolliver who gave valuable feedback and encouragement on a very early draft article which eventually grew into this text. Suzi Tucker, Managing Editor, did just that, managed and edited this text with skill and grace, and I thank her.

Thanks also to my colleagues D. Russell Crane, James M. Harper, Robert F. Stahmann, and Margaret H. Hoopes, all of whom have read and commented on parts of this text. I want also to acknowledge Ron Bingham who supplied me with much valuable information about new developments in supervision in the Association for Counselor Education and Supervision. And finally thanks to all my supervision students whose questions and comments are the reason for this text.

Effective Supervision
A Task-Oriented Model for the Mental Health Professions

Surveying the Field

INTRODUCTION

In surveying the field of supervision there are several questions one might wish answered. First, what is the definition of the field? Next, one might want to know something about the nature of therapists in supervision. Third, what is the role of the supervisor? And last, what variables, in addition to the supervisor, may influence the behavior of therapists in training. This chapter is designed to get us started finding some of the answers to these and related questions.

SUPERVISION AS A FIELD OF STUDY

If we are to establish supervision as a field of scientific study, several things must occur. The field must be defined, described, and critical variables must be determined through systematic research. The hope is that research will lead to the establishment of principles by which we can predict the outcome of specific supervision activities (Holloway & Hosford, 1983; Mead & Crane, 1978; Ryan, 1978). When we have identified supervision variables that lead to predictable changes in therapist behaviors, it will be necessary to show that the changes in therapist behavior are related to changes in client behaviors. Then, if the supervision variables that predict therapist changes can be manipulated, we can begin to control the supervision process in order to more consistently produce capable and competent therapists.

Defining Supervision

What are the outcome goals of supervision? At present the two top level goals of supervision appear to be to see that no harm comes to the clients (Loganbill, Hardy, & Delworth, 1982; Slovenko, 1980) and to increase the therapist's skill in delivering treatment to clients (Haley, 1988; Lambert, 1980). These goals begin to define the field of supervision. However, further specification is necessary to differentiate supervision from therapist education and related processes.

Bartlett (1983) states that a rather widely accepted definition of counseling supervision is "an experienced counselor helping a beginning student or less experienced therapist learn counseling by various means" (p. 9). Blocher (1983) defines supervision as "a specialized instructional process in which the supervisor attempts to facilitate the growth of a counselor-in-preparation, using as the primary educational medium the student's interaction with real clients for whose welfare the student has some degree of professional, ethical, and moral responsibility" (p. 27). Saba and Liddle (1986) provide a similar definition for supervision in family therapy: "the specific development of trainee's therapeutic abilities within the context of treating families" (p. 111).

The purpose of supervision is to change the behavior of trainees to resemble the behavior of an experienced expert therapist (Haley, 1988; Lambert, 1980; Wolberg, 1954). It is not expected that the therapist must become an expert, but it may be important that the supervisor provide an exemplar therapist as a model for the trainee to emulate (Gilbert, 1978). The goal of supervision is to help the trainee develop techniques that are effective and not detrimental (Bergin, 1971; Bergin & Lambert, 1978; Gurman & Kniskern, 1978). Taken together the five key elements in a definition of supervision appear to be (a) an experienced therapist, (b) safeguarding the welfare of the clients by (c) monitoring a less experienced therapist's performance (d) with real clients in clinical settings, and (e) with the intent to change the therapist's behavior to resemble that of an exemplar therapist.

The specification that supervision is concerned with the monitoring of the therapist's performance "with real clients in clinical settings" is one aspect that differentiates supervision from therapist education. Therapist education is concerned with the acquisition of knowledge about therapy and is usually achieved by means of texts, classroom lectures, seminars, and pre-practicum training (Bartlett, 1983; Blocher, 1983; Haley, 1988; Kagan, 1983; Patterson, 1983). Therapist education concentrates more on the therapist's performance on tests, whereas supervision is more focused on the therapist's performance with clients (Haley, 1988). Supervision is not therapist education, it is something else.

Supervision of therapy has traditionally been modeled on therapy;

however, supervision is not therapy. If supervisors operate on a model of supervision as a variant of therapy, the supervisor becomes a therapist and the trainee becomes a client. What then is the relationship of the therapist to the client? The therapist must put the welfare of the clients first. The supervisor has almost the same responsibility for the clients' welfare as the therapist (Slovenko, 1980). If supervision is therapy, then who is the client? The goal of supervision is to change novice therapists into expert therapists, not into expert clients. One does not learn to do therapy by undergoing therapy. Supervision is not therapy for the therapist, it is something else.

If supervision is not therapy for therapists and it is not therapist education, what is supervision? Supervision is the clinical preparation of novice therapists for the practice of therapy. In supervision the beginning therapist translates theories and concepts into performance. Successful supervisors guide the trainee's general professional development. Successful supervisors help their supervisees acquire, not only technical skills, but the ability to take independent action through the use of good clinical reasoning and judgment. Successful supervisors also help their trainees gain a personally integrated therapeutic style (Guest & Beutler, 1988; Stoltenberg & Delworth, 1987) that will sustain them throughout their professional lives.

The Nature of the Therapist's Experience in Supervision

It seems reasonable to assume that therapists' technical skills, capacity for independent activity, and personal therapeutic style will change over the course of supervision and training. Several questions are raised by this assumption. First, how are these differences in therapists' behaviors to be conceptualized and how are such differences to be determined and measured? Second, do therapists actually change in their response to therapeutic situations over the course of supervision and, if they do change, what are some of the characteristic differences in therapists' behaviors as they progress from novice to expert? And finally, if therapists' behaviors change over the course of training, do supervisors respond accordingly?

Conceptualizing therapists' skill levels. Assigning therapists to a particular skill level has generally been determined by the therapist's position in the educational or training hierarchy. That is, students in their first practicum are assumed to be at a beginning level, second practicum or second year students are assumed to be at an intermediate level, and students in an advanced practicum or in intern placement are assumed to be at advanced skill levels. This method of assignment has been a convenient way for researchers to establish groups of therapists assumed to vary in their skill levels. However, it should be clear that we are all beginners with regard to some skills and techniques, and that even beginners may have become expert at some skills prior to entering training and supervision. As a result trainees at any educational level may vary in their ability to deliver any given therapy technique. Therefore, more precise methods of defining and measuring therapists' skill levels should be developed.

Stein and Lambert (1984) point up some of the difficulties in establishing therapist levels. They note that experience and training are often confounded when researchers combine years of training with years of post-degree experience. They also note that therapist age is frequently confounded with experience in establishing therapist levels. Therefore, using the therapist's year in training as a method of classifying skill level may be misleading.

Another way of conceptualizing differences in therapist performance levels has been to describe the differences as developmental stages (Hogan, 1964; Loganbill et al., 1982; Stoltenberg, 1981; Stoltenberg & Delworth, 1987). Stoltenberg and Delworth (1987) provide an extensive review of the variables of age, experience, and learning as these variables specifically relate to developmental models of supervision. Only a brief review of the issues related to the use of the concept of development of supervision skills will be undertaken here.

True developmental variables are age specific (Kessen, 1960). Supervisor behaviors cannot be true developmental variables as they are not age specific. Therapists undertake supervision and training at almost any age from about 21 to 65, and most experience similar changes in their responses to the stimuli presented by contact with clients in clinical settings. Therefore, the changes in therapist behaviors in supervision are not a function of the therapist's age. Stoltenberg and Delworth (1987) conclude that age cannot be equated with developmental stages for therapists, as changes in therapist behavior are not due to age but rather to interaction of the individual with the environment.

Similarly, experience cannot serve as an explanation of developmental stages in therapist behaviors as experience is a function of therapist interaction with the environment over time and is not a function of time alone. Experience is defined as "knowledge, skill, or practice derived from direct observation of or participation in events" (Webster's, 1984). Therefore, experience alone could not lead to systematic uniform changes in therapist behavior as would be implied by developmental stages because experience, as defined, could as easily lead to diversity as to uniformity. The number of theories of human behavior and of psychotherapy that have been put forward in response to supposedly similar phenomena supports the latter hypothesis rather well.

Stoltenberg and Delworth (1987) point out that specific therapist behaviors cannot be equated with developmental stages, as specific behaviors may be learned independently from any given stage. Furthermore, stages that are formed on the basis of higher order tasks which are composed of lower order tasks are only descriptive and are, as a result, logically derived premises, not developmental stages (Stoltenberg & Delworth, 1987).

Rather than persist in the use of the term development or developmental to characterize changes in therapist behaviors during supervision, it is better to consider these as differences related to learning and the affective side effects of the supervision process. The term developmental levels suggests that the therapist skills reside somewhere inside of the individual engaged in becoming a therapist to be unfolded in response to the clients, the clinical setting, and the influence of the supervisor. However, the analysis above suggests that the changes in skills and the affective responses that frequently accompany exposure to the therapy environment are learned responses. By considering these changes as the result of learning we can be clearer about the nature and source of the variables that are important in the supervision process. Therefore, performance levels seems a more appropriate term than developmental levels to describe the changes therapists undergo as they move from novice to expert therapists.

A third way of conceptualizing therapists' responses over training has been to assign specific goals to be accomplished by therapists at various points in the training program. The goals are generally assigned on the basis of some model of therapy (Cleghorn & Levin, 1973; Tomm & Wright, 1979). Therapists' "progress" is then assessed against attainment of the skills expected at that stage in the training. The procedures and tasks so described are the "logically derived premises" noted by Stoltenberg and Delworth (1987). As suggested before, logically derived premises are descriptions of, not explanations of, therapist skills.

Stein and Lambert (1984) used several retrospective strategies to evaluate training and experience in the studies they reviewed. Others have begun to move to specify more clearly differences in therapist performance levels as they progress through supervision. For example, Pinsof (1979) used number of families treated plus supervisor ratings as a criterion for beginning and advanced skill levels. Some scholars have attempted to develop assessment instruments that evaluate therapist skills in specific areas (Allred & Kersey, 1977; Pinsof, 1979; Truax & Carkhoff, 1967) and others have attempted to assess therapists' overall skills (Breunlin et al., 1983; Harper et al., 1979; Mead et al., 1982; Piercy et al., 1983). Further research in assessment of supervision is needed. Accurate evaluation of the variables associated with supervision is important if we are to determine the effects of various supervisory interventions on therapists and ultimately on clients.

Therapists' responses to supervision. Research has shown that therapists vary, over the course of supervision, in the responses they give to questions related to the nature and type of supervision they prefer. Beginning therapists tend to respond that they value support and specific technical direction (Heppner & Roehlke, 1984). As therapists gain therapy experience, they indicate that they prefer supervisors who provide training in more complex and dynamic views of change (Heppner & Roehlke, 1984; Worthington, 1984a). More experienced therapists state that they prefer supervision that helps them establish a personal model of therapy (Worthington, 1984a). In similar studies Brock and Sibbald (1988) and Wetchler (1989) found that a mixed group of beginning and intermediate performance level marriage and family therapy trainees preferred supervision in which the supervisor implemented a mixture of didactic and experiential supervision. In other words, marriage and family therapy trainees also appear to prefer help with technical skills and to receive support from their supervisors.

After graduation, therapists' responses to questions about their therapy skills and performance tend to reflect the views they developed in training and reflect especially the views of their more influential supervisors (Guest & Beutler, 1988; Norcross & Prochaska, 1983). Walz and Johnson (1963) found that when therapists were asked to view video tapes of their therapy and then to rate (a) their client-therapist interaction and (b) their overall relationships skills, the therapists' ratings were similar to the ratings given by their supervisors. This appears to support Guest and Beutler (1988) in that therapists tend to model after their supervisors.

Guest and Beutler's (1988) review suggests that, in general, therapists prefer supervisors whom they perceive as experts. They also prefer that the supervisor's expert advice be delivered with acceptance and support. In contrast with Guest and Beutler's (1988) review, Heppner and Handley (1982) were not able to show a relationship between perceived expertise of student supervisors and the professional development of trainees. Perhaps the difference between the review by Guest and Beutler (1988) and Heppner and Handley's (1982) study was the use of student supervisors. The degree of expertise among student supervisors may not have been great enough to elicit detectable differences by the trainees.

In reviewing the literature, it appears that when therapists are asked what they prefer from supervisors and supervision they respond along two dimensions. They appear to be reflecting the therapy models that they have been or are being taught, and they seem to be expressing anxiety related to beginning work with actual clients (Borders & Leddick, 1987). Knowing they lack technical skills and fearing they may do some harm to clients, they seek help from supervisors in answering specific technical questions and support to manage their anxiety. After they have performed therapy for some time and have been reinforced for doing so, they are in a position to recognize increasingly subtle discriminating stimuli, and therefore, cases appear to take on more complexity. As a result intermediate trainees desire supervisors who provide training in more complex techniques and models, and who present a variety of methods that may serve as potential solutions to the therapy problems they are encountering. Once they have mastered the more complex techniques and models, more advanced trainees may feel some anxiety due to lack of organization or lack of integration among the various techniques and theoretical models. At this point they may seek supervision that helps them escape from the anxiety produced by their perception of disorganization or lack of integration. Therefore, advanced trainees may prefer supervision that fosters integration of the therapy theories they have learned into a personal model. Future research should be directed at determining if these or other variables are linked to the therapist's responses to questions related to their supervision preferences over the course of training.

Supervisors' responses to therapists' changes. If therapists' change their therapy skills and affective responses over the course of supervision, a related question is whether supervisors respond differently to therapists at various performance levels. The research is mixed on this issue. Yogev and Pion (1984) found that supervisors did not respond differently to first year trainees with no previous experience, to second year trainees, and to trainees with at least two years of previous clinical experience. Others (Loeber & Weisman, 1975; Miars et al., 1983; Reising & Daniels, 1983; Worthington, 1984a) have found that supervisor behaviors change as the therapists' performance levels change. In general, the findings suggest that supervisors provide the kinds of supervision therapists seek; technical information and support in the beginning, more complex technical training and a range of theoretical notions in the middle, and help integrating a personal theory at more advanced stages of training.

Role of the Supervisor

Stoltenberg and Delworth (1987) suggest that competent supervisors are characterized by the ability to assume a wide variety of roles as needed by their trainees. Supervision is similar to therapy and education in some ways, but supervision is a unique process that requires its own specific knowledge, skills, and attitudes. The role of the supervisor is briefly discussed here but will be discussed more extensively in the chapters that follow.

Conceptualizing the supervisor's role. What exactly should be the role of the supervisor? Hess (1980) has suggested five models of supervisor roles: (a) teacher, (b) case review consultant, (c) collegial peer, (d) monitor, and (e) therapist. Borders (Borders & Leddick, 1987) suggests that the role of the supervisor includes three relationship types; (1) counselor, (2) teacher, and (3) consultant. Haley (1976; 1988) suggests that the role of the supervisor might be to help the therapist identify solvable therapeutic problems related to cases on which the therapist is working. Haley's idea is similar to the consultant role set forth by Hess (1980) and Borders and Leddick (1987).

It seems likely that over the course of supervision most supervisors will use a number of roles as Stoltenberg and Delworth (1987) indicate. However, the role of consultant seems to fit most closely with the activities consistently described as being expected of supervisors. Beginning therapists appear to want supervisors to consult with them on specific techniques, therapists with intermediate skill levels want consultation on theoretical models for more complex problems, and more experienced therapists want consultation on integration of theory and techniques.

The computer systems analysts Coombs and Alty (1984) provide a description of the role of consultant that appears useful for therapy supervisors. Using Coombs and Alty's terms, the supervisor as consultant will observe the interaction of the therapist and the clients and will help the therapist to be clear and concise in ordering and describing the information related to the case. The supervisor as consultant will require the therapist to use good clinical reasoning and judgment in developing the treatment plan for the clients. When needed, the consultant role requires the supervisor to supply additional information or methods to the therapist to ensure that the clients are receiving adequate treatment. Finally, the consultant role requires the supervisor to monitor (a) the therapist's progress in delivering the treatment and (b) the therapist's skills in observing the impact of the treatment on the clients.

The consultant role for supervisors described above suggests the need for supervisors to be good observers of therapists and clients. However, Haley (1988) suggests that many supervisors do supervision without ever observing clients or therapists in therapy sessions. According to Haley this comes about because some models of supervision focus on the therapist describing the clients' problems to the supervisor whereas other models focus on the therapist's individual problems, that is, the supervisor acts as therapist to the therapist. It is not deemed necessary in either of these approaches for the supervisor to see the clients and the therapist in actual therapy interaction.

Haley's (1988) contention that much of supervision is done without the supervisor seeing the therapist in action is partially supported by recent research. McKenzie et al. (1986) found that 61 percent of the 550 supervisors surveyed used "written process notes" as their means of supervision and this was second to "listening to an audio tape," which was the most frequently used approach. Saba and Liddle (1986) reported similar findings in their study of marriage and family therapy supervision.

However, Haley's (1988) suggestion that supervision focuses on the therapist as an individual is not supported. In Brock and Sibbald's (1988) study of supervision in 14 marriage and family therapy training centers, 48 percent focused on therapist self-awareness "much of the time" or "as a total emphasis" and 50 percent gave therapist self-awareness as the focus only "some of the time" or gave self-awareness "no emphasis." Thus in Brock and Sibbald's study, supervision focused on therapist self-awareness in only about half of the training centers. In the much larger, and therefore possibly more representative study by McKenzie et al. (1986), "therapist interpersonal skills" was reported as sixth out of 12 possible responses and was, in fact, in a tie with "intervention techniques." The response "personal growth of the therapist" was ranked ninth. Saba and Liddle (1986) gave their respondents a list from which to select the focus of their training and supervision that included "therapist's personal issues, therapist-client relationship, skill-building, the case itself, and other foci." Their findings are difficult to interpret because they report that supervisors were given six choices: therapist's personal issues; therapist-client relationship; supervisor-therapist relationship; skill-building; the case itself; and other foci—however, they only report results for three of the cases. They report that supervisors used "skill building" most, followed by "case focus," and "therapist-client relationships." Saba and Liddle did not report the position of "therapist personal issues" but we can deduce that it was fourth or fifth. Taken together these studies give almost no support to Haley's contention that supervision centers on the individual development of the therapist to the exclusion of how to do therapy.

Perhaps most important of all, the role of supervisor as consultant is to provide support and encouragement. Trainees need support as they try out new therapist behaviors. Without support and reinforcement trainees may avoid trying techniques that are new or different. Trainees need support when their clients present them with problems that they are not fully prepared to treat. Without it they may not find therapeutic solutions to new problems they encounter. Support is necessary as trainees meet with clients who emit strong emotional behaviors. Without their supervisor's support, trainees may react to the strong emotions of their clients with counterattack, escape, or avoidance responses.

One of the best ways for supervisors to show support for therapists may be to act as a consultant and to leave the responsibility of the clients in the hands of the therapist as much as possible. The supervisor's primary responsibility is to consult with and support the trainee as she or he learns to be a therapist, but not to do therapy through the trainee.

An issue that is related to the role of the supervisor is the concern over whether a supervisor must be an experienced expert therapist in a specific model of therapy in order to teach that particular therapy model. Bordin (1983) and others (Goodyear & Bradley, 1983; Patterson, 1983) argue that supervision of a particular type of therapy must be given by an expert in that therapy. In contrast, Liddle (1988) states that the supervisor need not be an expert therapist to perform supervision. There does not appear to be any evidence in the literature to support either hypothesis. The issue seems open to empirical study. However, the more important issue may be whether the supervisor is an expert in helping therapists become better therapists. It may not be necessary for a supervisor to be an expert in every therapy technique that he or she teaches. The supervisor may provide exemplars of a technique by use of film or television tape, or by having a therapist, who *is* an expert, model a technique "live." Ethically, it appears necessary that the supervisor takes care to supervise within his or her boundaries of competence. The supervisor must be proficient enough in a technique to be able to determine that the trainee is delivering treatment that is not harmful to the clients.

Supervisors' responses in supervision. What supervisors do in supervision may be a function of performance level rather than a function of their expertise in a given therapy. Worthington (1984c) found that more experienced supervisors tend to attribute therapist behaviors to situational variables whereas less experienced supervisors tend to attribute therapist behavior to therapist traits. Stone (1980) found that experienced supervisors generated more planning statements about trainees than did those with less experience. Holloway and Wolleat (1981) found that the behavior of beginning supervisors varies between sessions for individual trainees. They also found that behavior varied among beginning supervisors. In another study Holloway and Wampold (1983) report that for student supervisors the most significant behaviors provided were supportive communications, asking for information in response to questions from therapists, and being defensive or critical in response to critical or defensive remarks made by the therapists. All of the above responses were devalued by the therapists, the supervisors, or both. In an earlier study, Holloway (1982) indicated that beginning supervisors do not use an effective strategy to elicit an increase in the therapist's ideas about therapy. These findings suggest that beginning supervisors, like beginning therapists, lack both technical skills and an integrated model of supervision.

These studies seem to indicate that inexperienced supervisors need help in developing technical skills to elicit better clinical thinking in therapists. Inexperienced supervisors also need help in learning not to counterattack therapists who make mistakes, make difficult inquiries, or who criticize the supervisor (Holloway & Wampold, 1983; Stoltenberg & Delworth, 1987). The studies also suggest that beginning supervisors must be supplied with a model of supervision. This model should facilitate consistency among sessions and consistency among student supervisors. The purpose of this text is to provide beginning supervisors with a model of supervision which will fulfill these needs.

Other Variables Related to Supervision

If we consider the factors in the clinical setting that are likely to control a therapist's responses to clients, we can see that, in addition to the supervisor's behavior, there are four other classes of variables.

As noted by Mead and Crane (1978) there are: (a) the clients' behaviors; (b) the setting variables, such as the consulting room, the one way mirror, television cameras, and the presence or absence of one's peers behind the mirror; (c) the therapist's personal history, including his or her preferred model of therapy; and (d) the administrative constraints established by the training institution or the agency in which the therapist works. These variables are called contextual variables by Liddle, Breunlin, and Schwartz (1988) and social context by Haley (1988).

In addition to the four classes of variables mentioned above that may impinge more or less directly upon the therapist as he or she attempts to practice therapy, there are other variables mentioned by Liddle, Breunlin, and Schwartz (1988) and Haley (1988) that probably exert less direct influence. This class of variables may be referred to as cultural variables. Some examples of cultural variables are the various professional organizations and their codes of ethics; political and legal issues; the feminist movement; and issues related to race and ethnicity. At this time little research has been conducted to determine the impact of contextual and cultural variables on the processes or outcomes of supervision and training in therapy.

SUMMARY

It has been suggested that supervisors and administrators who establish training programs should take into consideration the changes that occur in therapists over the course of the program (Borders & Leddick, 1987; Guest & Beutler, 1988; Stoltenberg & Delworth, 1987). Supervision procedures should vary according to the skills of the therapists and their affective responses to training settings and experiences. Training is best facilitated by beginning with nonspecific areas such as establishing a working relationship, and developing communication skills (Crane, Griffin, & Hill, 1985). At this level of training, supervisors should be highly credible and should maintain a warm and supportive atmosphere (Stoltenberg & Delworth, 1987). The supervisor should model a clear and direct form of therapy that helps therapists solve problems with their clients (Haley, 1988).

As therapists achieve an intermediate level of skill, they should be introduced to a variety of models and emphasis should be on the conceptual differences among the models as related to behavior change (Guest & Beutler, 1988). Specific theories may be taught focusing on specific technical skills such as teaching parents and couples communication skills, problem solving skills, and specific techniques in cognitive restructuring (Bootzin & Ruggill, 1988). During this time the supervisor may assume more of a role of teacher and authority according to Stoltenberg and Delworth (1987).

At the advanced level of training, which appears to occur at about the level of the therapist's post-master's supervision or the doctoral student's internship training, supervision should focus on the therapist's personal attributes in therapy and the development of the therapist's personal style of therapy. According to Guest and Beutler (1988), supervision may center on issues of transference and countertransference and further consolidation of the therapist's communication and technical skills. Supervisors at this level may assume the role of case consultant.

As therapists continue their lifelong process of becoming educated as therapists, they continue to improve their technical skills and add new techniques through reading, attending workshops, and professional meetings. Supervision at this level of therapist experience comes through collegial peer relationships and exchanges (Guest & Beutler, 1988).

As a basis for assisting therapists making the changes described above, the supervisor must have a consistent supervision model of (1) the procedures and tasks required of clients in therapy, (2) the interaction of therapists and clients in therapy, and (3) the interaction of supervisors, therapists, and clients. Such a model will provide a guide to the variables surrounding therapists' performance of (a) observation, (b) information gathering and processing, (c) clinical judgments and decision making, (d) treatment planning, (e) treatment delivery, and (f) assessment of progress and outcome. It is the goal of this text to provide the supervisor with such a model.

CHAPTER 2

A Task-Oriented Model of Supervision

INTRODUCTION

This chapter attempts to define and describe the procedures used by supervisors in the mental health fields. Because the procedures are used by most supervisors, regardless of the model of therapy or model of supervision the supervisor uses, they are considered "general" procedures. The amount of emphasis given to any one of the procedures will vary from supervisor to supervisor but it appears that each of the tasks is required to get the job of supervision done. Therefore, the procedures described make up the minimum set of supervision tasks required.

The theoretical antecedents for the Task-Oriented Model come from behavioral principles, the work in computer sciences related to expert systems, and the literature of supervision. The assumptions from behavioral theory are that the variables that govern the supervisor's behavior may be discovered in the supervisor-therapist-client system (Mead & Crane, 1978). Inasmuch as these variables are open to manipulation, these variables can be used to predict and eventually control the supervisor's and the therapist's behaviors. Discovering the variables that control the behavior of supervisors should eventually result in better trained therapists and, ultimately, better therapy for clients.*

*It should be noted that behavioral tasks are part of behavioral theory but not necessarily part of behaviorism. We are concerned here with the behavior of supervisors, therapists, and clients as they interact with each other to create a supervisor-therapist-client system. The members of

The assumptions from computer sciences and expert systems research are that the strategies and tasks performed by supervisors are not theory specific. That is, in the performance of supervision, the tasks and operational procedures performed by a client-centered supervisor do not differ in kind from the procedures performed by an existential supervisor, a brief therapy supervisor, a psychodynamic supervisor, and so on (Halsing, Clancy, & Rennels, 1984). The tasks and procedures that all supervisors must perform are, therefore, "general" procedures.

Both the expert system approach and the behavioral approach require that the procedures and tasks be described as clearly and explicitly as possible. The attempt in this text is to make the operational performances and tasks used by supervisors as explicit as possible. The results are sure to be a crude description of the intricate behavior of supervisors. However, as Skinner (1957) notes, even a crude beginning may lead to improvement in the behaviors under study and crude beginnings may be refined by others which in turn lead to further improvements.

Definitions Revisited

In Chapter 1 we define supervision as "an experienced therapist safeguarding the welfare of clients by monitoring a less experienced therapist's performance with the clients in a clinical setting with the intent to change the therapist's behavior to resemble that of an experienced expert therapist." This definition points to several specific supervisory processes related to the therapist's behavior such as "monitoring" and "intent to change." It also points to an important goal. The goal is to change the therapist's behavior to resemble the behavior of "an experienced therapist." However, the definition offered is by no means a model of supervision. A triple systems model of supervision is needed to explain the behavior of the supervisor and the behavior of the therapist as they work together in the three systems relevant to the supervision domain: (a) the therapist-client system, (b) the supervisor-therapist system, and (c) the supervisor-therapist-client system (Breunlin, Liddle, & Schwartz, 1988; Tomm & Wright, 1982; Wright & Coppersmith, in press).

It is widely held that supervision can best be described as an exten-

---

these systems exchange behavior by means of which they control the behavior of the other members of the system. These behavior exchanges exist in the physical world and can be observed, assessed, and manipulated. The reciprocal exchange of these behaviors constitutes a social system.

sion of therapy (Goodyear & Bradley, 1983; Holloway & Hosford, 1983; Leddick & Bernard, 1980; Liddle, Breunlin, & Schwartz, 1988; Patterson, 1983). As a result of this perspective, many current descriptions of supervision are labeled by the theory from which they were derived. In addition many scholars believe that the model of therapy being taught can only be taught by experts in that model (Fisch, 1988; Mazza, 1988; Patterson, 1983).

Recently some scholars have come to see supervision as an activity that is distinct from therapy and therapy education, although they would not deny that there are elements of therapy and education in supervision (Bartlett, 1983; Bernard, 1979; Blocher, 1983; Holloway & Hosford, 1983; Littrell, Lee-Bordin, & Lorenz, 1979; Loganbill, Hardy, & Delworth, 1982; Mead & Crane, 1978; Russell, Crimmings, & Lent, 1984; Ryan, 1978; Stoltenberg & Delworth, 1987). The model of supervision as an activity independent from therapy and therapist education is the approach taken in this text.

Therapy, Theory, and Supervision
The idea that supervision is an extension of a particular therapy theory and that supervision must be conducted by a therapist who is an expert with that theory places a severe limitation on supervision and supervisors. One of the limitations of a supervision theory derived from a single therapy theory is that no model of therapy has been shown to be capable of treating all of the problems presented by all clients in therapy. Therefore therapists, to be successful, must be eclectic in their treatments. As a result supervisors must be prepared to supervise eclectic therapists in performing treatments that may not be derived from the supervisor's model of therapy. In order to be effective, supervisors must be expert supervisors in addition to being successful therapists (Liddle, 1988; Russell, Crimmings, & Lent, 1984; Stoltenberg & Delworth, 1987).

Expert supervisors should be capable of helping their trainees with most clinical treatments regardless of the theory from which the treatment was derived. This probably can be best accomplished if the supervisor is an expert clinician rather than an expert in one therapy theory.

An expert clinician may be defined as a therapist who has mastered most of the technical skills and who has developed an integrated personal clinical model of therapy. A clinical model of therapy is an eclectic approach based upon empirically tested treatments. Empirically tested treatments are those that have been shown to be effective with specific groups of clients with specific problems. A clinical eclecticism differs from the more common form of eclecticism in that it is based upon a critical, reasoned, objective examination of treatments rather than treatments that simply fit the therapist's personal preference (Brabeck & Welfel, 1985).

Expert clinicians make use of theory to (a) determine what information is important to collect; (b) organize and conceptualize the information as it is collected or once it is collected; and (c) formulate treatment plans logically based upon the information that is known. Thus expert clinicians can move from theory to the specific information, from the specific information back to theory, and back again to specifics (Burr, Mead, & Rollins, 1973). Supervisors who are expert clinicians should be well prepared to supervise trainees in treating the full scope of problems presented by clients in therapy.

In addition to being expert clinicians, supervisors need a model of supervision that is independent of therapy models. Supervisors need a model of supervision that will help them supervise either a specific model of therapy or supervise a therapist with a model of supervision that differs from the model of the supervisor. Supervisors require a model of supervision that will aid in the supervision of trainees who are eclectic clinicians treating the specific needs of their clients with the clients' present set of problems. One such model of supervision is the Task-Oriented Model. The Task-Oriented Model is designed to help supervisors who are expert clinical therapists help trainees to become expert at performing clinical therapy.

Changing therapists' behavior. Our definition of supervision states that the goal of supervision is to change the therapist's behavior to resemble that of an expert therapist. Bernard (1979) indicates that supervisors characteristically take on one of three roles in their effort to change therapists, that of teacher, counselor, or consultant. The definition of supervision used here combines elements of all three but defines the role of supervisor differently.

The role of the supervisor is to change the behavior of therapists. The supervisor does this by arranging experiences or interventions that will change the therapist's responses to clients in clinical sessions. As Lambert (1980) has noted, these interventions may take different forms such as "instruction, supervisor modeling, direct observation, intervention by the supervisor in the actual process . . . and feedback from direct observations or with audio/videotape recordings" (p. 425). Supervision is, first and last, an activity that is designed to change therapist's interaction with clients in clinical sessions in such a way that the therapist's interaction is therapeutic for the clients.

Supervision and case consultation. A distinction may be made between the functions of supervision and case consultation (Kaslow, 1977; Loganbill, Hardy, & Delworth, 1982). In supervision the supervisor has the responsibility to evaluate the therapist's performance and to take action that will directly impact upon other areas of the therapist's life, such as continuing in an academic program or receiving promotions and pay raises in a job setting. The ethical implications of such dual roles is discussed in Chapter 9.

In other situations the supervisor may function more as a consultant to the therapist. In consultation the consultant may have the responsibility to point up the therapist's strengths and weaknesses but may lack the power and authority to require changes in the therapist's behavior or to impose sanctions for noncompliance. However, it appears that except for the power to require compliance and impose sanctions there are very few differences in the processes of supervision and consultation. Both require the application of the supervision skills described in this text. Therefore, no further distinction will be made between supervision and consultation.

A TASK-ORIENTED MODEL FOR SUPERVISION

The Task-Oriented Model focuses on three systems that can be seen in terms of levels and meta-levels (see Figure 2.1). Level 1 is the client system level. This level provides a model of the general procedures and tasks to be performed by clients in conjunction with the therapist as the clients move through therapy. Level 2 is the therapist level. This level describes the procedures and tasks that must be executed by therapists as they perform therapy. Level 3 is the supervisor level. Level 3 describes the tasks to be performed in supervision. All three levels are hierarchically connected in the process of supervision.

The events on Level 1 do not occur, for most clients, without the action of the therapist at Level 2, that is, for example, clients' marital problems do not appear to remit without therapy (Coyne, 1986; Hahlweg & Markman, 1988). The reciprocal interaction between the therapist's behavior at Level 2 and the clients' behavior at Level 1 creates the therapist-client system. Therefore, Level 2 is hierarchically superior to, or meta to, Level 1.

The behavior of the supervisor is hierarchically superior to the be-

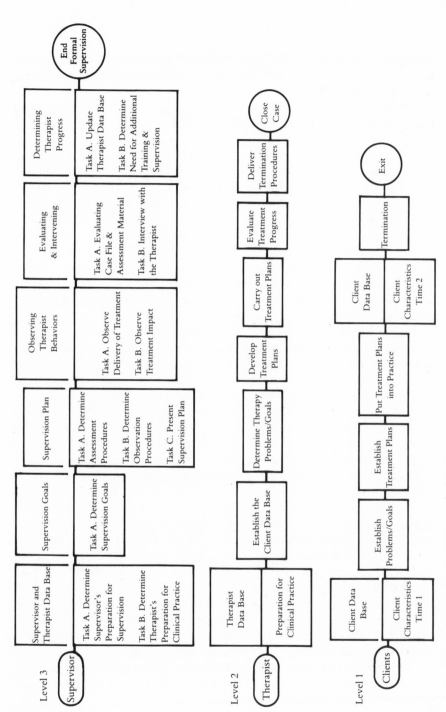

Figure 2.1 Task-Oriented Model of Supervision

Level 3

Supervisor

| Supervisor and Therapist Data Base | Supervision Goals | Supervision Plan | Observing Therapist Behaviors | Evaluating & Intervening | Determining Therapist Progress |

Task A. Determine Supervisor's Preparation for Supervision

Task B. Determine Therapist's Preparation for Clinical Practice

Task A. Determine Supervision Goals

Task A. Determine Assessment Procedures

Task B. Determine Observation Procedures

Task C. Present Supervision Plan

Task A. Observe Delivery of Treatment

Task B. Observe Treatment Impact

Task A. Evaluating Case File & Assessment Material

Task B. Interview with the Therapist

Task A. Update Therapist Data Base

Task B. Determine Need for Additional Training & Supervision

End Formal Supervision

Level 2

Therapist

Therapist Data Base

Preparation for Clinical Practice

Establish the Client Data Base

Determine Therapy Problems/Goals

Develop Treatment Plans

Carry out Treatment Plans

Evaluate Treatment Progress

Deliver Termination Procedures

Close Case

Level 1

Clients

Client Data Base

Client Characteristics Time 1

Establish Problems/Goals

Establish Treatment Plans

Put Treatment Plans into Practice

Client Data Base

Client Characteristics Time 2

Termination

Exit

havior of the therapist in supervision, thus Level 3 is meta to Level 2. The supervisor's and therapist's interaction makes up the supervisor-therapist system.

By extension, the supervisor level, Level 3, is not only meta to the therapist level but also to the client level. Therefore, interaction between supervisor and therapist concerning the behaviors of the clients forms the supervisor-therapist-client system (Breunlin, Liddle, & Schwartz, 1988; Wright & Coppersmith, in press). Taken together this complex arrangement of levels, meta-levels, and overlapping systems make up the supervision domain. It is this domain that is modeled and explained in the Task-Oriented Model of supervision. The three levels are discussed next, but first a word or two of warning.

Whenever we diagram procedures, as in Figure 2.1, the procedures appear linear and multidimensional. Supervision certainly is multidimensional but it is hardly ever linear. The process might better be modeled with the new nonlinear mathematical models being used to describe chaotic or transition events (Gleick, 1987).

In the supervision process, as with most chaotic phenomena, several of the processes described in Figure 2.1 are happening at the same time, although the processes often have their own independent time scales with some moving fast and some moving more slowly. Within each level and between the levels the processes loop and branch in several directions. The events do not always come in the order pictured and, although the flow is generally in the left to right direction, over time, it is possible for the processes to fold over themselves and for tasks to be repeated several times before moving on to the next. For example, the therapist may believe she or he has collected enough information to form a client data base from which to develop the treatment plan until the supervisor points out a missing piece of information. Then the therapist must loop back from treatment planning to data gathering. At the same time the supervisor is revising his or her assessment of the therapist's preparation for independent practice based upon this new evidence of therapist competence. Note too that the supervisor would not be able to make accurate changes in his or her understanding of the therapist's behavior without accurate information about the client's behaviors. The supervisor must be able to move quickly and freely among all three levels.

Although supervision processes are chaotic or nonlinear this does not imply that they are unpredictable. Each of the members of the supervision domain may provide stimuli to the other members.

These reciprocally exchanged stimuli act as reinforcement, punishment, or discriminative stimuli that increase the probability of some behavior on the part of the participants. The supervisor's job is to help the therapist understand the probabilities implied by the clients' behavior and the probable outcomes for client behavior that may follow from the therapist's responses to the clients. The supervisor must also keep in mind that he or she is inputting certain stimuli into the supervisor-therapist-client system and that eventually the therapist must become self-supervising, providing appropriate responses without the direction of the supervisor.

It is clear then that Figure 2.1 vastly oversimplifies the supervision domain. Nonetheless a simple description, as stated earlier, gives us a place to start understanding the processes of supervision and provides the basis for future revisions. To further help us understand the model each of the levels of Figure 2.1 will be described briefly.

The Client Level

The client level in Figure 2.1 depicts the processes the clients pass through in the course of therapy. Although clients may pass through these steps without the aid of the therapist, it appears that for some disorders, such as marital dysfunction, the probability is that they will not be successful (Coyne, 1986; Hahlweg & Markman, 1988). The various models of therapy, such as psychoanalytic, client-centered, behavioral, rational-emotive, and structural-strategic family therapy, are essentially models of how clients pass through these steps in the process of treatment.

From the point of view of a Task-Oriented Model, clients enter therapy with a set of characteristic behaviors and interaction patterns that they have acquired from their genetic histories, their extended family interaction histories, their individual personal histories, and their interaction histories as a couple or as a family of procreation. It should be noted that although clients share some of their history with other members of their family and with other members of the culture at large, still each client's history is unique. Each client's history forms a data base that is more or less accessible to the client and, it is hoped, to the therapist.

As a function of the individual data bases each client formulates his or her perception of the problem and its probable solution. Each client comes to therapy with some ideas for making the problem "go away." Clients may come to therapy with some more or less specific goals that they hope to achieve. They expect the therapist to come to understand the given problem just as they do and to do some sort of intervention that will help them resolve it. Once that is done clients expect to be able to leave therapy changed for the better.

Level 1 may be considered a "general" model of the clients' behavior in therapy. That is, the Task-Oriented Model of therapy described in Level 1 of Figure 2.1 embraces the various theories of therapy. As a general model of therapy the Task-Oriented Model may help overcome problems encountered when the supervisor's and the therapist's paradigms clash.

The supervisor may use the model provided at Level 1 to structure the therapist's use of any of the theories of therapy. By observing the clients, the supervisor can determine which client task the therapist needs to work on to move therapy ahead. Then by knowing the therapist's model and goals for the session, the supervisor can determine if the therapist's actions or proposed actions appear to be congruent with the task to be accomplished.

Clearly, for successful supervision to occur the supervisor must be active at all three levels of the Task-Oriented Model, observing the clients, the therapist, and executing the tasks of the supervisor. For example, if the therapist is attempting to apply behavioral theory and the therapist has just been assigned the case, the supervisor may ask, "What information do you need to collect from this client, according to behavioral theory?" If the therapist is at an intermediate level of skill, the supervisor might follow the previous question with, "What other theories might apply to this case and what information would they suggest you collect?" For advanced therapists the supervisor might ask, "How do you conceptualize this case and what information do you plan to collect?"

The Task-Oriented Model sets the stage for clinical supervision. Once the significant information is gathered the supervisor may ask, "How do you conceptualize this case, given the information that you now have?" When the therapist responds, the supervisor might pose the question, "What additional information is needed and how can you collect it most efficiently?" When the supervisor believes that the therapist has all the relevant information, she or he might probe further, "What other conclusions could one come to, given this information?" and then, "What information is needed to confirm or disconfirm any of these hypotheses?" Here the supervisor is using the steps in the Task-Oriented Model to elicit and evaluate the therapist's clinical reasoning. The supervisor can continue to elicit responses, or encourage the therapist to go back to the clients to gather more information, or suggest that the therapist take some appropriate action to test out the hypotheses. The supervisor's choice of action is based upon the supervisor's information related to the client and therapist levels.

The Therapist Level

The therapist comes to supervision with a personal and professional history. The therapist's personal history is constructed just as is each client's individual history. That is, therapists have acquired a set of characteristic personal behaviors from their genetic histories, from their interactions in their extended and nuclear families, and from their individual experiences all of which have become a part of their history. However, similarities between the therapist's personal history and the personal histories of the clients are usually purely coincidental.

The therapist also comes to therapy with a professional history. The therapist's professional history incorporates reading of professional literature, attendance in various courses, experiences in therapy role play, and previous clinical practice. The therapist interacts with the clients on the basis of his or her personal and professional history. Therefore, it is important for the supervisor, as well as the therapist, to be aware of the relevant aspects of the therapist's history (Liddle, 1988; Mead & Crane, 1978; Stoltenberg & Delworth, 1987).

The boxes on Level 2 labeled "Therapist Data Base" and "Preparation for Clinical Practice" are there to suggest that the therapist has had some preparation for therapy and that the therapist has that information available at varying levels of awareness. Therapists will vary widely in their ability to articulate their history (Borders & Leddick, 1987). Consequently, helping therapists to clarify and specify their readiness to do therapy is one of the tasks of the supervisor (see Figure 2.1, Level 3).

The remaining boxes at Level 2 describe the general procedures a therapist uses to help clients resolve their problems or reach their goals. Just as Level 1 is a general theoretical model of client behavior, Level 2 is a general model of therapist behavior. Recently several authors (Liddle, 1988; Stoltenberg & Delworth, 1987) have put forth developmental models of therapists' changes in ability to carry out therapy procedures. Liddle (1988) and Stoltenberg and Delworth (1987) describe systemic and developmental theory based models of the changes in therapists' skills as they proceed to conduct therapy under supervision. The Task-Oriented Model describes the skills that are general for all models of therapy. Therapists must be able to execute the skills at Level 2 of the Task-Oriented Model if they are to perform as expert clinicians.

It is assumed that these skills are used by therapists regardless of their theoretical persuasion, although specific skills will receive more emphasis in one theoretical group than in another. The tasks specified in the Task-Oriented Model that all therapists need to be able to perform are as follows.

The therapist interacts with the clients and begins to extract selected parts of the clients' histories. What is selected is partially a function of the therapist's theory of client behavior. On the basis of these inter-changes the therapist begins to formulate a partial data base for each client. The client data base models the client's behavior, his or her characteristic ways of interacting with others and the environment.

Using the information gathered from the client, the therapist uses clinical reasoning to structure a number of hypotheses about the client's problems and goals. Some of these hypotheses can be sup-ported or eliminated based upon the data available; some may require gathering additional information before they can be tested. When the therapist is convinced that enough information has been collected to clearly describe the client's problems and goals, the therapist again uses clinical reasoning to formulate a treatment plan.

The treatment plan is put into action by the therapist. The therapist begins to deliver the treatment interventions stated and implied in the treatment plan. The hypotheses about changes in the client's behav-iors, which were derived from both the therapist's theory of client behavior and change, and from the therapist's sampling of the client's behaviors at Time 1, are then tested. This is done by the therapist doing an evaluation of the client's characteristic behaviors at Time 2 and comparing them with the client's behaviors at Time 1. Time 2 is some point during or after the treatment interventions. If the prob-lems that the client brought to therapy have dissipated, or the goals that the client came to therapy to achieve have been reached at Time 2, the therapist terminates the case and closes the case file. If the problems have not been resolved, or the goals have not been achieved, the therapist may loop back to sample more of the client's data base to further clarify the problems and then repeat the steps above.

Therapists may vary in their ability to execute, in the presence of clients, the therapist skills on Level 2 of the Task-Oriented Model. They may lack the technical skill to apply the procedures with a given type of client, with particular types of problems, and in specific settings. They may be unable to relate the various skills to a theory of therapy or to show how the skill relates to several different theories. Or they may be unable to describe their efforts to utilize these skills from the point of view of an integrated personal model of therapy.

By identifying the tasks that are causing difficulty, the supervisor will be in a position to offer interventions that may help the therapist improve her or his clinical skills. Paradigm clashes are avoided when supervisor and therapist work together to identify the tasks to be accomplished and how the various theories can contribute to their accomplishment.

As the supervisor monitors the therapist's ability to carry out Level 2 tasks with the clients, he or she intervenes with support and corrective feedback as needed. The specific tasks of the supervisor are described next.

The Supervisor Level

Level 3 of Figure 2.1 describes the general procedures supervisors use to carry out supervision. As said earlier, the tasks described in the Task-Oriented Model appear to be the minimum number of steps required to implement successful supervision.

The supervisor must determine the therapist's preparation for clinical practice. For a beginning therapist this may mean overall preparation. For a more experienced therapist it may mean preparation to perform a specific technique with which she or he is not familiar, such as how and when to use systematic desensitization, how to plan an indirect intervention, or how to do creative relabeling.

The information concerning preparation is partially known to the therapist as part of the therapist's data base (Borders & Leddick, 1987). The supervisor must access this information from the therapist and form for himself or herself a data base of the therapist's readiness to engage in therapy. "Readiness" means both ready to begin performing the tasks described in Level 2 of the Task-Oriented Model and having the structural skills suggested by Stoltenberg and Delworth (1987). These skills include the ability to differentiate self from others and the ability to act independently across the therapy domains of (a) intervention, (b) assessment, (c) interpersonal interaction assessment, (d) case conceptualization, (e) ethnic, gender, and racial issues, (f) theoretical orientations, (g) treatment plans, and (h) professional ethics.

Before assigning cases to the therapist, the supervisor needs to meet with the therapist to determine the goals of supervision. Once the goals are determined, the supervisor will establish how he or she will observe the therapist's progress. A supervision plan is then established which details how feedback will be delivered during supervision and how the therapist will be evaluated (Borders & Leddick, 1987).

The supervisor then proceeds to observe the therapist delivering therapy and determines the effectiveness of the therapist's efforts, including the effects upon the clients. Next the supervisor determines the therapist's perceptions of her or his treatment delivery, the impact of that treatment on the clients, and the therapist's clinical reasoning about the case. Finally, the supervisor provides feedback to the therapist or takes other action to help the trainee become a more effective therapist and to intervene on the clients' behalf, if necessary.

After this cycle has been repeated with a variety of clients and with a full range of clinical problems, the supervisor evaluates the therapist's competence and determines with the therapist the need for additional training. If more training is needed, the cycle is repeated. Otherwise the therapist ends formal training and is free to take a position among his or her professional colleagues. It is hoped that one outcome of this process is a therapist who will continue to be self-educating and self-supervising.

As suggested above many supervisors use a model of supervision that is derived from their personal theory of therapy. This may limit the supervisor, as such models generally lack a model of the supervisor's behaviors and provide no information about the role of the supervisor in relationship to the therapist and the clients. Taken together Figure 2.1 is a general model for supervision and as such it covers all of the essential systems for conducting therapy supervision, the client system, the therapist-client system, and the supervisor-therapist-client system (Breunlin, Liddle, & Schwartz, 1988; Wright & Coppersmith, in press). The chapters that follow detail the specific tasks required of supervisors to carry out the procedures that are outlined in Figure 2.1 and described briefly above. However, before delving into the tasks of supervision it is important to review the supervisor's data base—the supervisor's preparation to do supervision.

The Supervisor's Preparation for Supervision

The supervisor comes to supervision with a personal history that is determined by his or her genetic, family, and individual background. The professional history includes the supervisor's preferred theory of therapy and the supervisor's model of supervision. Taken as a whole, the supervisor's history is the supervisor's preparation to do supervision.

Supervisors need preparation to do supervision just as therapists must be prepared to do therapy (ACE, 1988; Borders & Leddick, 1987; AAMFT Commission on Supervision, 1989). Specifically, supervisors need to have competence in (a) the technical skills of supervision, (b) conceptualizing the events occurring on all three levels of the supervision domain—the client level, the therapist–client level, and the supervisor–therapist–client level, (c) the theories and research related to supervision, (d) ethical and legal issues related to supervision, and (e) developing an integrated personal model of supervision (AAMFT Commission on Supervision, 1989).

Preparation in the technical skills for supervision includes perceptual and executive skills which, as described above, will assist the supervisor in (a) determining the therapist's preparation for therapy, (b) establishing supervision goals, (c) establishing methods of observing and assessing the therapist's therapy, (d) preparing a supervision plan, (e) carrying out the observation of the therapist's treatment delivery and the impact of that treatment on the clients, (f) evaluating and intervening to help the therapist become more effective, and (g) determining the therapist's progress toward becoming an expert therapist.

Preparation for conceptualizing the events of supervision requires the supervisor to have a model of supervision that will assist him or her in relating to the therapist's approach to the clients, the model of therapy being taught, and the several other models of therapy, including the supervisor's preferred model. Therefore, preparation for supervision requires that the supervisor has an understanding of several models of therapy and the research that supports the clinical application of principles from those theories to specific types of clients, with specific problems.

Preparation for conceptualizing the processes of supervision also necessitates that the model of supervision take into account the client system, the therapist–client system, and the supervisor–therapist–client system (Breunlin, Liddle, & Schwartz, 1988; Wright & Coppersmith, in press). The Task-Oriented Model presented here should help the supervisor integrate the various models of therapy across the three systems in the supervision domain.

Preparation in the theories and research related to supervision is achieved by study of the supervision literature. Many clinical programs provide a course that surveys the literature. Such a course will serve as an introduction to supervision and may serve as the catalyst for the supervisor's lifelong search for understanding and knowledge of how people become expert supervisors.

A supervisor begins to develop an integrated personal theory of supervision through the study of various models of supervision and related research. Then, by the processes of clinical reasoning, the supervisor begins to formulate a model of supervision that he or she can apply with a variety of therapists who are seeing a variety of clients, with a wide array of clinical problems. This model is tested in the field through application in clinical settings as the supervisor goes about the business of helping therapists become more expert. The problems that the supervisor encounters lead to revisions of the supervisor's model and the process continues.

ASSESSING THE SUPERVISOR'S READINESS FOR SUPERVISION

Before beginning to do supervision, it is important for the supervisor and the supervisor-of-the-supervisor to determine the supervisor's preparation (Borders & Leddick, 1987; Breunlin, Liddle, & Schwartz, 1988; Liddle, 1988; Stoltenberg & Delworth, 1987; Wright & Coppersmith, in press). The "Professional History: Preparation for Supervision" form (Appendix A) was designed to assist marriage and family therapy supervisor-trainees and supervisors-of-supervisors to determine readiness for supervision. A similar form for use by supervisors and therapists of individual therapy may be found in Borders and Leddick (1987).

Evaluation of Supervision

There has been some debate over whether supervision should be evaluated by assessing change in the therapist or change in the clients (Goodyear & Bradley, 1983; Hansen, Pound, & Petro, 1976). Given our definition of supervision, it should be clear that it cannot be a case of one or the other. Supervision must ultimately be evaluated by assessing events on all three levels of the Task-Oriented Model. The behavior of the supervisor must ultimately be assessed by determining the impact of the supervisor's behavior on the therapist, which in turn, influences the behaviors of the clients. Therefore, the first question to be asked is, did the therapist's performance in sessions with clients change as a result of the supervisor's interventions? Next it must be determined if the changes in therapist's behavior in sessions with clients result in in-session and out-of-session behavior changes by clients (Kagan, 1983; Lambert, 1980; Matarazzo, 1978).

It would appear that it is important to use both changes in therapists' in-session behavior and changes in client behavior as dependent variables of supervision. Only when we can point to specific cause and effect relationships among supervision practices, therapist behaviors, and client outcomes, will we begin to have a science and technology of supervision.

Assessing Changes in Supervision Skills

From the discussion above it is apparent that supervision assessment must take place at all three levels of the Task-Oriented Model. It is also generally understood that a multi-person and multi-method approach to assessment of interpersonal interaction provides the most complete picture of the events of interest. Recently there have been three reviews of assessment techniques for determining changes related to supervision (Borders & Leddick, 1987; Holloway, 1984; Stoltenberg & Delworth, 1987). These scholars present an array of assessment techniques that take advantage of the fact that supervision lends itself very well to a multi-person approach to assessment.

Supervisors who wish to evaluate their performance can use self-report ratings, the ratings of their trainees, and the ratings of their supervisors. In addition clients' self-reports of their interaction and of their relationship with their therapists and clients' perceptions of the impact and outcome of the therapy may be gathered. Supervisors may video tape their sessions with their trainees and these taped sessions may be coded by trained coders. It is well known that correlations between the methods of assessment tend to be low. Nonetheless the various approaches provide different views of the phenomena of supervision which can be useful for evaluating one's progress in gaining and using supervision skills.

Following are brief descriptions of some assessment instruments that may be used by supervisors alone for self-evaluation, some instruments that may be administered to trainees to evaluate the supervisor's performance, and some instruments that have parallel forms and may be administered to both supervisors and trainees to compare the supervisors' perceptions with the perceptions of the trainees. Finally, some observation rating methods that have been used to evaluate supervisor behavior are briefly discussed.

The "Professional History: Preparation for Supervision" form (Appendix A) which was described previously may be used by marriage and family therapy supervisors for self-evaluation. A similar form, "Competencies of Supervisors" by Borders and Leddick (1987), may be used by individual therapy supervisors. The Developmental Level Determination Scale (Wiley, 1982) has a supervisory environment subscale that assesses supervision environments related to the three trainee developmental (performance) levels postulated by Stoltenberg (1981). The Level of Supervision Survey (Miars et al., 1983) also assesses the supervisor's perception of supervision environments related to Stoltenberg's supervision levels.

For trainees to evaluate supervisors, the Counselor Development Questionnaire (Reising & Daniels, 1983) consists of two subtests that are designed to measure the trainee's perception of a number of trainee variables—such as anxiety and independence—and a number of perceived supervisory needs—for example, emotional consultation and skills training. The Critical Incidents Questionnaire (Heppner & Roehlke, 1984) asks trainees to describe critical incidents in their supervision. The Supervision Checklist (Rabinowitz, Heppner, & Roehlke, 1985) lists critical incidents in supervision and asks trainees to select the seven most important supervisory interventions used by their supervisor. The Supervision Assessment Scale (Hart, 1982) may be employed to evaluate the frequency of supervisor statements about the client's personality dynamics, therapy techniques, and the supervisor-trainee relationship.

With respect to instruments that have parallel forms to be administered to both the supervisor and the trainee, the Counselor-Orientation Questionnaire (Loesch & McDavis, 1978) may be used to measure the therapist's and the supervisor's preferences for seven major theoretical therapy orientations (Friedlander, Siegel, & Brenock, 1989). The Session Evaluation Questionnaire (Stiles & Snow, 1984) can be used to measure the immediate impact of a supervision session. It has been employed to test parallel relationships in interview sessions that take place between supervisor-therapist, and therapist-client (Friedlander, Siegel, & Brenock, 1989). The Supervision Perception Form (Hepppner & Roehlke, 1984) is designed to assess supervisors' and trainees' perceptions of the impact of the supervisor on the trainee's therapy skills and their perceptions of the trainees' willingness to learn from the supervisor. The Supervision Questionnaire (Worthington & Roehlke, 1979) measures both the supervisor's and the trainee's perceived importance of various supervisor behaviors. A factor analysis of the Supervision Questionnaire found two independent variables that were named evaluation and support. The Supervisor Emphasis Rating Form (Lanning, 1986) uses parallel forms to assess the skills the supervisor keys on during supervision. The Supervisor Personal Reaction Scale (Holloway & Wampold, 1983) is used to evaluate both the supervisor's and the therapist's performance plus the level of comfort each experienced in expressing his or her own ideas.

Some observation rating methods that have been developed to observe the supervision process are as follows. Blumberg's Interactional Analysis was adopted by Holloway (1982) to measure interpersonal interactions between supervisors and therapists. The Relational Communication Control Coding System (Friedlander, Siegel, & Brenock,

1989; Heatherington, 1988) is a coding scheme that may be used to identify dyadic and triadic (Friedlander & Heatherington, 1989) verbal communications as interpersonal influence attempts. The Interpersonal Communication Rating Scale (Strong, 1987; Strong & Hills, 1986) is employed to code messages reflecting status traits and affiliation needs of the sender. The Supervisory Feedback Rating System (Friedlander, Siegel, & Brenock, 1989) is used to code supervisor verbal behavior into feedback or nonfeedback. Feedback is then analyzed into four dimensions, (a) type, interpersonal or cognitive-behavioral; (b) specificity, global or specific; (c) valence, positive or negative; and (d) focus, the therapist–client relationship or the supervisor–therapist relationship.

Supervisors, supervisors-of-supervisors, and researchers who wish to find ways to improve supervision may chose from this array of assessment devices and methods to evaluate supervision processes and methods. The instruments listed will allow assessment from the level of the supervisor, the therapist, or an observer. Information about the process of supervision may be augmented to determine the impact of supervision by assessing the behavior of the therapist and the clients' responses to the treatment delivered by the therapist. Ultimately, a multidimensional approach of this sort will provide considerable information concerning the methods and processes of supervision.

This chapter has presented a broad description of a Task-Oriented Model of supervision. The chapters that follow present more detailed descriptions of each of the specific tasks.

CHAPTER 3

Establishing a Therapist Data Base: Determining The Therapist's Preparation for Clinical Practice

INTRODUCTION

The first task of the supervisor is to determine the therapist's preparation for clinical practice, that is, to establish the therapist data base. In the first meetings with the trainee, the supervisor seeks to establish a working supervisory relationship in addition to establishing the therapist's preparation for therapy. As part of the process of establishing a supervisory relationship, the supervisor begins by sharing with the therapist his or her qualifications for doing supervision, the nature of the supervision that will be offered, the supervisor's general expectations for the therapist, the methods of supervision that will be used, and how the therapist's progress will be evaluated. The therapist should be informed that in the first two or three meetings they will determine in detail the therapist's preparation for supervision, the therapist's goals, the supervisor's specific goals, and the methods and procedures to be used to achieve those goals. Therefore, the purpose of the first supervision meetings will be to arrive at a mutually acceptable plan for supervision.

Introducing the Supervisor to the Therapist

Although many of the details concerning supervision expectations and methods will be worked out in later sessions, it is important to attend to a number of relevant issues in the first session. One of the tasks to be achieved in the first session is the introduction of the supervisor to the therapist. This exercise in self-disclosure may serve several purposes. It is one step in establishing the supervisor-therapist working relationship. It sets a precedent for the self-disclosure required from the therapist as the supervisor and therapist work together to establish the therapist's preparation for therapy. And it is a model for the therapist to use in his or her initial therapy sessions.

The supervisor should be prepared to explain his or her preparation and qualifications for doing supervision based upon the supervisor's self-review (Appendix). Student supervisors should share the fact that they are supervisors-in-training and that they will be supervised by an experienced supervisor. It is also appropriate to discuss your supervisor-of-supervision's qualifications briefly. This discussion leads naturally to issues of confidentiality.

Introducing the Therapist to Supervision

Confidentiality. Confidentiality in supervision focuses on two major areas, the confidentiality of client information and the confidentiality of the information about the therapist that becomes known to the supervisor. The obligations of confidentiality about client information do not change as that information is shared in both the therapist-client relationship and in the supervisor-therapist-client relationship. However, risks to confidentiality increase with the number of persons involved. Therefore, special care must be taken to limit the number of people exposed to confidential client information. It is imperative that the supervisor has access to the client information, especially with new, less experienced therapists. However, it is not at all clear how much confidential client information is needed by the supervisor of the supervisor. There appears to be no empirical guidance on this issue and there is little theory. Consequently, the best that can be said may be that all parties involved are under an obligation to uphold the highest standards of the code of ethics and to use good professional and clinical judgment.

As supervision is not therapy, the rules of confidentiality that apply to the therapist-client relationship may not apply to the supervisor-therapist relationship. Therefore, it is important that the supervisor clarifies to the therapist what will be the limits of the confidentiality of the information shared between them. Discussion of the limits should be shared in the first session to prevent the therapist from unwittingly disclosing information that may later be communicated by the supervisor to others.

The issue of confidentiality and the therapist's risks in disclosing to the supervisor differ from those of a client disclosing to the therapist in that the supervisor may have the responsibility to evaluate the therapist. The supervisor is often called upon to evaluate the therapist's performance and to report any progress or lack of progress to other faculty members, agency administrators, and/or to the therapist's advisor in the therapist's home institution. The issues related to evaluation should be discussed as part of the discussion of confidentiality so that both parties are aware of the role the supervisor must play. In the course of this discussion the supervisor should model the processes of good communication, giving the therapist the opportunity to respond both intellectually and affectively to the issues.

Supervision procedures. Discussion of the nature of the supervisor's role in supervision can be an important part of establishing a good working relationship with the therapist. It also serves as a basis to begin specifying and clarifying some of the procedures that will be part of the supervision process. For example, it can be explained that this is one of the places where supervision and the supervisor-therapist relationship is clearly different from therapy. A discussion on other ways supervision differs from therapy can follow. Additional procedures to be clarified in the first session include the number and length of supervision sessions to be held and where and when they will take place (Borders & Leddick, 1987). It is a good idea to also discuss what to do between supervision sessions should an emergency arise. The supervisor should tell the therapist how and where he or she can be contacted in an emergency and what to do if the supervisor cannot be reached.

The supervisor should also describe briefly, in the first session, the nature of the supervision to be provided. Any specific theory or techniques that the therapist will be expected to master should be brought up. Arrangements for observation and feedback should be shared including expectations for live supervision (observation through a one-way screen), video or audio taping of sessions, and reviewing of the therapist's case notes. The supervisor should provide the therapist with instructions on how to prepare for observation and supervision sessions, such as any special preparation of tapes or case notes.

It is also a good idea to discuss the procedures to be used in therapist evaluation. The supervisor's expectations for evaluation and the expectations of the agency or agencies involved should be stated, and the number and timing of evaluation periods and the criteria to be used should be mentioned. Methods of evaluation whether by verbal feedback, grades, or written evaluations of strengths and weaknesses should be described. If the evaluation will be passed to others, such as the therapist's home institution advisor, this should be communicated to the therapist in the first session.

Related to the issue of evaluation is the issue of site visits by representatives of the home institution (Borders & Leddick, 1987). Will there be site visits? If so, how many and when? What will the supervisor and therapist be expected to do in preparation for these visits? If there are to be site visits, it is probably a good idea for the home institution representative to meet with the therapist and supervisor during one of the early supervision sessions so that everyone's expectations can be clarified before the supervision plan is written up.

Borders and Leddick (1987) also suggest discussing client assignments. The therapist needs to know what types of clients she or he might expect over the course of supervision, the number of clients that can be anticipated, and what will happen if there are too few clients. The trainee may also want to know if she or he can have a say in the assignment of clients. Other issues concerning clients should be discussed, such as whether or not fees will be assessed and if they are, how collection will be handled.

Much of this information could, and perhaps should, be described in a handout to be given to the therapist, either prior to entering supervision or at the first supervision session. However, the written information should not just be given to the therapist without the provision of an opportunity for discussion. The supervisor should make time to discuss the issues with the therapist to allow the therapist to clarify the expectations and procedures. Talking about these issues can contribute greatly to the development of the supervisor-therapist working relationship.

Establishing a Supervisor-Therapist Working Relationship

In order to determine the therapist's competence to do therapy, the supervisor must first establish a collaborative working relationship with the therapist-trainee. This process is similar to that used to establish rapport with a client or join with a family in therapy. The supervisor must demonstrate care and respect for the therapist and a genuine interest in the therapist's welfare.

The supervisor demonstrates care and respect by being open and direct in describing the supervisor's qualifications, the nature of the supervision, and the supervisor's expectations for the trainee. Respect for the therapist can also be demonstrated by inviting the therapist to take part in developing the supervision plan. During the first session, the supervisor can explain that the therapist will have the opportunity to share his or her goals for supervision and to negotiate the details of the supervision process before the supervision plan is completed. The supervisor can explain further that only after the supervisor has compiled a data base of information about the therapist's skills and qualifications for doing therapy will they agree on a supervision plan. This process will take two or three sessions, after which the supervisor will prepare a written supervision plan (Borders & Leddick, 1987).

Establishing the Supervisor's Therapist Data Base

The supervisor's therapist data base consists of all the information the supervisor can bring together about the therapist's preparation for clinical practice. This information is known to the therapist at some level of awareness (see Figure 2.1, Level 2) but must be discovered by the supervisor. The information the supervisor seeks is the therapist's knowledge of therapy theories, techniques, and skills, and his or her ability to apply that knowledge with clients in clinical sessions. In addition, the supervisor needs to assess the therapist's motivation for doing therapy and for learning additional therapy skills, techniques, and concepts.

Assessing the Therapist's Preparation for Clinical Practice

Before assigning clients to the therapist, the supervisor needs to determine, in collaboration with the therapist, the therapist's preparation for doing therapy. The supervisor first must assess the therapist's overall readiness to do therapy. Second, assessment is required of the therapist's preparation (a) to perform the specific clinical techniques demanded by the treatments to be executed during this period of the therapist's training, (b) to use the specific theoretical model being applied in this training setting, and (c) to interact with the clients who are typically seen in this setting.

Assessing the therapist. After the supervisor has shared his or her qualifications as a supervisor and after the supervisor has begun to set the boundaries and rules to be used in supervision, the supervisor and therapist begin to work together to determine the therapist's qualifications to do therapy. Together they need to determine if the therapist has the skills to elicit relevant information from the clients concerning their problems and their goals for therapy. Together they must determine that the therapist can conceptualize that information according to theoretical principles and form an integrated picture of the clients and their problem. They need to determine that the therapist can develop a treatment plan based upon: (a) the information gathered; (b) relevant theory; and (c) good clinical reasoning. It is necessary that they determine if the therapist is prepared to keep the clients' issues and affective responses separate from the therapist's issues and affective responses while delivering the treatment as specified by the theory and the treatment plan (Shaw & Dobson, 1988). Finally, the ways by which the supervisor will evaluate the therapist's progress in acquiring and delivering therapy skills over the course of supervision should be discussed.

Trait versus state views of therapist competence. How the supervisor approaches therapist evaluation may be a function of whether the supervisor sees therapist behavior as a trait emanating from within or as a state which is a function of external conditions. Whether the supervisor views the therapist's skills as a trait or state will determine, in part, the way she or he sets about to evaluate therapist competence.

The trait view of a therapist suggests that the qualities needed by a therapist are either innate or learned over a lifetime. The personal traits needed by therapists as listed by Sakinofsky (1979) sound like the qualifications for sainthood, "He must already be a concerned, compassionate, intelligent, and sensitive human being before his training even begins. Training may mature and refine the experience of his concern and empathy, but it cannot supply what does not exist in the first place" (p. 195). This would suggest that in establishing the therapist data base the supervisor must determine if the trainee has these qualities.

There are several ways the supervisor may assess the therapist's intelligence, concern, compassion, and sensitivity. First, these qualities may be evaluated, as is frequently done, by the trainee's self-report (Shaw & Dobson, 1988). Second, the supervisor may make his or her own subjective profile of the therapist's traits, perhaps on the basis of the therapist's interactions with the supervisor. Third, assessment of the trainee's traits may be done by various standardized instruments such as intelligence tests, for example the Graduate Record Examination, and scales designed to rate the trainee's concern, compassion, and sensitivity such as the Barrett-Lennard Relationship Inventory (Barrett-Lennard, 1962). The Barrett-Lennard Relationship Inventory is designed to measure therapist's use of empathy, congruence, and unconditional regard which may be regarded as a measure of compassion and sensitivity.

If therapist competency is viewed as a state, competency is seen as a collection of behaviors that are influenced by the trainee's preparation, the clinical setting, the behavior of the clients, the behavior of the supervisor, and administrative issues (Mead & Crane, 1978; Shaw & Dobson, 1988). From this point of view, the supervisor's job in determining the trainee's readiness to perform therapy is to evaluate the therapist's skills.

It is assumed that the therapist comes to supervision with certain verbal skills designed to prepare him or her for the delivery of some forms of psychotherapy. The therapist's verbal skills have been developed by the therapist's study of the therapy literature, by his or her attendance at therapy lectures, and by participation in therapy discussions. These verbal skills were most likely tested by oral or written examinations. It may also be that the therapist has had the opportunity to try these skills in role playing and simulated situations and that these performances were monitored and feedback was provided. Thus prepared, the therapist is considered ready to begin practicing therapy.

As with the assessment of therapist traits, several methods are available to the supervisor to evaluate therapist skills. The supervisor may simply ask the therapist for a self-evaluation or the supervisor may have the trainee complete a self-report inventory such as Sections I, and II, and III of the "Professional History: Preparation for Supervision" form (Appendix). As already mentioned, self-evaluation is a typical approach to the evaluation of clinical competence (Shaw & Dobson, 1988).

Stoltenberg and Delworth (1987) and Borders and Leddick (1987) provide lists of instruments that may be used to assess relationship and individual therapy skills. Liddle, Breunlin, and Schwartz (1988) provide a list of assessment instruments to assess family therapy skills. Some of the instruments that have been developed to evaluate therapists' preparation appear to be theory or technique specific. Unless the supervision to be provided corresponds with the material assessed by that instrument, assessment methods that are tied to a specific theory may have limited usefulness for determining that therapists are ready to begin practice with the specific theories to be taught, by this supervisor, at this time, with the types of clients typically seen in this setting.

Instruments that were designed to evaluate a range of therapy skills are available. The Barrett-Lennard Relationship Inventory (Barrett-Lennard, 1962) mentioned earlier measures skills that are seen as fundamental to most therapies as do the Hill Counselor Verbal Response Category System (Hill, 1978) and the Inventory of Counselor Behaviors (Dustin et al., 1982). These latter instruments assess general skills such as use of approval and praise, open or closed questions, confrontation, explanation, and reflection. Piercy et al. (1983) have developed an instrument to consider general family therapy skills called the Family Therapist Rating Scale (FTRS), which is designed to assess five categories of family therapist skills. The five categories are said to represent the work of almost the entire range of theorists doing family therapy. The skills are structuring, relationship, historical, structural/process, and experiential. However, Piercy et al. (1983) fail to include an evaluation of behavioral skills.

Other methods of evaluating skills include observation and rating of the trainee's performance in role playing or simulated therapy sessions using other trainees acting as clients, coached clients, or video taped enactments. In addition, the supervisor may observe and rate the trainee's work with real clients. Although ratings can be made by the supervisor, if valid and reliable ratings are needed, it is necessary to have the rating done by independent and trained judges. Several authors have put forward coding systems (Allred & Kersey, 1977; Ericson & Rogers, 1973; Heatherington, 1988; Patterson, 1985; Pinsof, 1979; Rogers, 1979). However, coding systems are expensive in terms of training time for coders and the time required of therapists and supervisors. Consequently, coding by trained raters is rarely used except in research studies.

Assessing the therapist's conceptual skills. Therapist conceptual skills have been singled out by a number of scholars as critical to the therapist's ability to do therapy (Cleghorn & Levin, 1973; Tomm & Wright, 1979). Therapist conceptual skills are those skills used in the determination of what client behaviors to observe and assess, what hypotheses are formed by the therapist from the information that he or she has gathered, and the treatment plans that follow from those hypotheses. The conceptual skills appear to be a function of the therapist's model of therapy, the therapist's technical skills for gathering information, and the therapist's ability to organize and use all of this information to form hypotheses and treatment plans that are appropriate for the clients' behavior and interaction.

Assessment of the therapist's conceptual skills may take several forms just as the assessment of technical skills does. The supervisor can ask the therapist for a self-evaluation of conceptual skills. A self-report of conceptual skills may be more difficult for the therapist to give than a self-report on technical skills. Conceptualization requires that therapists be able to maintain a large amount of fairly discrepant information in their heads and be able to manipulate that information to respond in new, meaningful ways. Self-reporting about such behavior may be rather unreliable.

Perhaps the most effective way to observe therapists' ability to conceptualize about cases is to present them with a case and to ask them to describe their behavior as they proceed. The case may be role played by other trainees or by coached clients, or the case may be simulated on video tape or video disk. The assessment case may also be one of the therapist's current cases. The supervisor can probe for the therapist's conceptualization skills by asking a number of questions such as those found in Figure 3.1 or by use of techniques found in Kagan's Interpersonal Process Recall (Kagan, 1980) or the work of Bernstein and associates (Bernstein, Hofmann, & Wade, 1986; Bernstein & Lecomte, 1979a).

Several scholars have developed assessments for evaluating therapist conceptualization. Breunlin et al. (1983) report measuring conceptual skills by asking the trainee to describe behavioral data observed on a video tape. According to Stoltenberg and Delworth (1987), the Oetting-Michaels Anchored Ratings for Therapists (Michaels, 1982) assesses behaviors related to interviewing, conceptualization, and sensitivity to client and trainee issues. Other assessment instruments for measuring therapist conceptualization and cognitive processes related to therapy include the Intentions List (Hill & O'Grady, 1985), the Clinical Assessment Questionnaire (Holloway & Wolleat, 1980), and the Written Treatment Planning Simulation (Butcher, Scofield, & Baker, 1985). These latter instruments are reviewed in Borders and Leddick (1987).

Assessment of therapist's skill performance levels have been undertaken by numerous scholars. Stoltenberg and Delworth (1987) and Borders and Leddick (1987) review a number of assessment instruments designed to determine the therapist's performance or experience level.

UNDERSTANDING THE PROBLEM

First

You have to understand the problem.

What is the desired outcome?

What does each person want from therapy? What behaviors would each person like to see increase? decrease? What conditions link what is happening here and now to the desired outcomes? Is it possible to satisfy these conditions? Can you write down the outcomes? The conditions?

What are the data?
Can you put the data in order? Can you write it down? Can you diagram the data? Are there patterns in the data? What pre- post-tests can be administered? What continuous measures can be used? Continuous recording? Direct measurement of permanent product? Event recording? Duration recording? Interval recording? Time sampling?

What are the conditions?

Can you separate the various elements of the conditions presented by the clients? Can you write them down? Can the problem be treated (solved) by our current techniques and skills? If not, how many inventions such as new techniques, would be needed to solve the problem?

DEVISING A PLAN

Second

Find the connection between the data and the desired outcome.

Do you know of any treatments for related problems?

Have you seen it before? Or have you seen the same problem in a different form? Do you know a tested treatment program for this problem? For a similar problem?

Consider the desired outcomes.

Try to think of a familiar problem having the same or a similar set of desired outcomes.

(continued)

Figure 3.1. Solving Therapy Problems

Reorder the data.

Could you use a method from another treatment program? Should you introduce some auxiliary element in order to make the tested treatment program possible? Can you restate the problem in other words? Could you restate it still differently? Can you redefine the terms of the problem? If you cannot treat the proposed problem can you treat first some related problem? For example, a more general problem? A more specific one? An analogous problem? Can you treat part of the problem? Can you get the clients to keep only part of the conditions (values, attitudes, automatic responses, etc.), drop other parts; how close does this bring you to the desired outcomes? Can you see anything useful in the data? How can it vary? What variables control the current behavior? What variables control the desired outcome behaviors? Can you think of other data appropriate to reach the desired outcomes? Does everyone agree on the definitions?

Did you use all the data? Did you explore all of the conditions?

DEVELOPING A TREATMENT PLAN

Third

You should eventually arrive at a treatment plan.

What are your hypotheses?

What variables are controlling the clients' current behavior? What variables may control the desired outcome variables? How can these variables be changed? By the client? By others in the client's family, friends, fellow employees? Might there be other controlling variables? How can you discover them? What new hypotheses might they suggest?

What conceptual frameworks are you employing to tie together the data? What other concepts fit this data? What hypotheses do they suggest?

What are the theoretical principles you are using to organize your concepts? What competing theories can you think of to organize these concepts? Do these suggest new hypotheses? Can you list all the possible hypotheses which may relate to this data? Which hypotheses can you eliminate based on the data at hand? What additional data would you need to get to eliminate the next most plausible hypothesis? Does this suggest an intervention? A series of interventions?

Write out your treatment plan.

State all your hypotheses, including all the competing ones, in writing.

Write out your proposed treatment plan in enough detail so that a reasonably competent therapist could take over the treatment if necessary. Indicate your criteria for success or failure of the therapy. Spell out how the data to determine progress and success will be gathered. Indicate possible decision points where treatment may be altered. Describe any possible side effects. Estimate the amount of time necessary to reach the goals.

Share your treatment plan with your clients and obtain their agreement and commitment.

CARRYING OUT THE PLAN

Fourth

Carrying out your treatment plan, check each step.

Carry out your plan.

Are the steps too large for the clients? Too small? Do the clients see how each step relates to the final desired outcomes? Can you see clearly that the steps are correct? Does the data suggest need for altering the procedures?

LOOKING BACK

Fifth

Are you ready for case termination?

Examine the outcomes obtained.

Does each member of the family feel they have reached the desired outcomes? Does each feel that they are getting their needs met in the system? Does your data give evidence that the treatment you applied made the difference? Can you use the result or method for some other problem?

Evaluating the therapist's preparation for doing therapy in a specific setting. Beyond assessing the therapist's general preparation, the supervisor needs to determine that the therapist is prepared for the specific tasks she or he is about to undertake. To evaluate the therapist's preparation for practicing psychotherapy in this specific setting, the supervisor may present the therapist with a list of specific classes of problems likely to be encountered in that setting. The use of lists to assist the therapist in self-reporting about his or her specific therapy skills speeds up the process of evaluation by serving as prompts for both therapist and supervisor (Hill & O'Grady, 1985; Mead, Valentine, & Gay, 1987). Lists also help to ensure that all critical areas are included.

The list of problems the trainee is likely to encounter in a given setting should include the most prominent classes of cases seen in that clinic, for example, depression, families with conduct disorder children, and marital distress. Within any specific problem class, the therapist may be given additional lists of sub-skills related to treatment, such as initial interview procedures, assessment procedures, specific treatment procedures used with the given class of problems, specific factors that contraindicate the use of any specific treatment, and specific interventions that make up the treatment of choice for that specific problem class.

From these lists the therapist identifies specific classes of problems that he or she has mastered at the level of verbal or conceptual skills (Cleghorn & Levin 1973; Tomm & Wright, 1979) and perhaps at the level of prepracticum training. Areas where the therapist is less prepared can also be identified. In this way therapist and supervisor can quickly determine how well prepared the therapist is to begin to do therapy in this particular setting.

Therapist education and self-education. If, after inspecting the lists of client problem classes required to do therapy in this setting, the therapist and supervisor turn up gaps in the therapist's preparation, then the supervisor must direct the therapist to the pertinent theoretical and empirical literature. At this point the supervisor slips out of the supervision domain and into the therapist educator domain (Bernard, 1979).

By teaching the therapist to recognize where his or her knowledge and skills are deficient as well as how to use consultation and the professional literature, the supervisor is teaching the therapist to become self-educating. It may be pointed out that continued reading and the gaining of experience with new techniques are necessary throughout one's professional career. Once formal education has been completed, information concerning new techniques and concepts can be found in the journals. In addition, the therapist may gain experience and practice in using new techniques by attending workshops (Shaw & Dobson, 1988) or by visiting sites where new techniques have been developed and are being taught.

As mentioned earlier in this chapter, not only must the supervisor identify the therapist's preparation for therapy, but she or he must also determine the therapist's motivation for therapy and for supervision. Thus, while exploring the therapist's preparation for clinical practice, the supervisor can also be assessing the therapist's motivation toward the profession, toward the theory being taught, and toward being a trainee.

Determining the Therapist's Motivation

Motivation for therapy refers to the factors that influence someone to engage in therapeutic behaviors. Motivation for supervision also refers to the variables that increase the probability that one will engage in the supervision process.

In trying to discover the therapist's motives for doing therapy or for taking part in supervision, we are searching for the controlling variables. We might ask what variables are likely to increase the probability of this therapist behaving in a therapeutic way with clients and what variables are likely to reduce the probability that he or she will continue to engage in therapeutic behavior? We might also ask about variables that will cause this therapist to respond to supervision favorably or at least without punishing the supervisor. What variables will cause the therapist to react to supervision with some behavior other than escape and avoidance? Considered in this way, therapist motivation for clinical practice is a function of the therapist's reinforcement history, the therapist's current state, and the current schedule of reinforcement and punishment provided by the supervisor (Skinner, 1953).

Some have suggested that therapists are motivated by a variety of goals (Greenberg, 1980; Liddle, Davidson, & Barrett, 1988; Loganbill, Hardy, & Delworth, 1982; Stoltenberg & Delworth, 1987). Goals are outcomes that have a history of being reinforcing (Skinner, 1989). Expectations appear to be similar to goals. One's expectation of reinforcement is a function of past reinforcement for similar classes of behavior (Skinner, 1989).

Others have suggested that therapist motivation is a function of needs. Needs and drives relate to states of deprivation and satiation (Skinner, 1953, 1989). For example, therapists who have for any reason been deprived of the opportunity to help other people may begin helping others at the first opportunity to do so. Such therapists may be described as "having a need" to help others. On the other hand, therapists who have spent long hours for weeks and years helping others may experience "burn out," which is a form of satiation on therapy.

Fear, anxiety, and punishment also appear as motives in therapy supervision. Therapists are said to fear exposing "personal, interpersonal, cognitive, and professional inadequacies" (Liddle, 1988, p. 154). Performance anxiety is said to be typical of beginning therapists (Borders & Leddick, 1987; Liddle, 1988; Stoltenberg & Delworth, 1987). Past experiences with evaluation may have proven punishing, and therefore, the anticipation of evaluation may induce anxiety.

Inasmuch as therapist and supervisor are able to assess the therapist's motivation for performing therapy, they may be able to manipulate the variables related to the therapist's anxiety and thus be able to control the therapist's motivation for therapy and supervision. While the supervisor should work to provide a relatively nonpunishing environment to reduce fear and anxiety, the supervisor must simultaneously establish conditions that will encourage the therapist to try new procedures and to conceptualize his or her work in novel ways.

Assessing therapists' motivation. Drawing from our analysis above, assessing motivation for therapy and supervision appears to be best approached from the point of view of assessing the therapist's goals, expectations, needs, fears and anxieties, and punishment history. Assessing the therapist's goals will be discussed at length in the next chapter.

The subject of assessment of therapist needs in supervision has been addressed by several scholars (Reising & Daniels, 1983; Stoltenberg, Pierce, & McNeill, 1987). For example, Stoltenberg and Delworth (1987) state that beginning therapists "have a greater need for supervisor-provided structure and positive feedback than do the more advanced trainees" (p. 60). They base this assertion on the findings by Stoltenberg, Pierce, and McNeill (1987) in which beginning therapists score higher in response to items that indicate a desire for structure, instruction, positive feedback, and support from their supervisors. However, the use of the word "needs" by these researchers actually appears closer to goals and expectations than needs. Needs are responses that can be shown to have a functional relationship to states of deprivation and satiation. Therapists may express the desire for instruction and structure to avoid the punishment of performing poorly. They may want positive feedback and support as evidence that they have not performed poorly and are not going to receive punishment. Therefore, the therapist's requests for structure, instruction, positive feedback, and support may be more a function of histories with reinforcement and punishment than with states of deprivation and satiation. They may be expressing anticipatory avoidance responses due to fear and anxiety more than they are expressing needs.

Therapist fears and anxiety may be assessed as part of the affect related to supervision. The Environment Scale of Wiley's (1982) Developmental Level Determination Scale is reported to assess the affective aspects of supervision (Stoltenberg & Delworth, 1987) as does Reising and Daniels' (1983) Counselor Development Questionnaire. Punishment that may be occurring in the therapist's therapy sessions or in supervision sessions may be assessed using coding systems designed to evaluate specific target behaviors. For example, client resistance may be coded to determine if client behavior is punishing for the therapist (Heatherington, 1988; Heatherington & Friedlander, 1987; Patterson, 1985). Worthington and Roehlke's (1979) Supervision Questionnaire appears to be a self-report approach to assessment of punishment in supervision sessions. The Supervision Questionnaire is designed to assess supervisor evaluation and support. The evaluation scale may be a measure of punishment in supervision.

At a more global level therapist motivation for supervision may be evaluated by use of the Supervisor Perception Form which was developed by Heppner and Roehlke (1984). The Supervisor Perception Form is reported to measure supervisory impact and willingness to learn. The willingness to learn scale may be a measure of motivation as it is said to assess the trainee's openness and receptivity to the supervisor's suggestions and directives.

SUMMARY

Determining the therapist's preparation for clinical practice starts with the supervisor. The supervisor determines his or her preparation for supervision and shares his or her preparation, style, and expectations with the therapist in the first meeting. The supervisor establishes the basic format to be used and begins the process of evaluating the therapist's skills and techniques, methods of conceptualizing clients, and motivation for therapy practice. This process may take two or three sessions. Although some measurement techniques are available to assist the supervisor, the most common process for determining therapist skills at this time is through the therapist's self-reports. Once the supervisor and therapist have some common understanding of the therapist's basis for doing therapy, they are ready to establish the goals for supervision.

CHAPTER 4

Determining the Supervision Goals

INTRODUCTION

There are several reasons to establish goals for supervision. First, making a good beginning is an important part of supervision (Liddle, 1988) and establishing clear, specific, and achievable goals is one way to accomplish this. Second, the cooperative effort required to establish mutually agreeable goals for supervision is an important part of facilitating the working supervisor-therapist relationship. The process can foster mutual respect and develop mutual commitment to the course of supervision (Borders & Leddick, 1987). Third, goals that are spelled out in achievable steps can be an important source of motivation (Borders & Leddick, 1987). Fourth, in settings where evaluation of the therapist is required, clear and specific goals can facilitate the evaluation process. Finally, the process of defining clear and specific goals for supervision provides a model to the trainee defining goals in therapy.

Written Supervision Goals

Just as it is good practice to have written treatment goals for therapy (Fowler & Longabaugh, 1975; Tomm & Sanders, 1983), it is good practice to have written supervision goals. Supervision practice will undoubtedly be improved by having specific and concrete goals clearly delineated. Written supervision goals will make the evaluation of the therapist's progress easier (Borders & Leddick, 1987; Loganbill et al., 1982), and written goals will make it easier for the supervisor to determine appropriate supervisory interventions.

Written goals are most conducive to good communication (Fowler & Longabaugh, 1975) and good communication should improve the process of supervision. Good communication is considered to be important in building relationships and the supervisor-therapist relationship is seen by many as the critical ingredient in the supervision process (Hess, 1980; Hutt, Scott, & King, 1983; Lambert, 1980; Loganbill et al., 1982; Schwartz, 1988).

Written supervision goals are a crucial part of the supervision plan and a well-written supervision plan may well be the key to more effective supervision practice and research. The steps to writing supervision goals are described here and a discussion of the completed supervision plan is presented in Chapter 5.

Written supervision goals appear to have three principal components: (a) clearly stated, observable outcomes; (b) specific action steps to reach the goal; and (c) specific procedures to evaluate the outcomes (Borders & Leddick, 1987; Mager, 1972). The steps for writing goals that Mager (1972) recommends are:

- Write the goal in general abstract language.
- Write a list of all words and actions someone would perform that would cause an observer to say that he or she had achieved the goal.
- Edit the list for duplications and for abstract and general terms.
- Test the list by asking, "If someone did all that, would you agree that they had achieved the goal?"
- Write out a complete statement of the goal.

The process of writing goal statements is the same whether the supervisor is writing them for the therapist or the supervisor is asking the therapist to write his or her own. Each of these components of supervision goals is described below.

Stating supervision goals. Supervision goals should be stated in clear, specific, and observable terms, rather than being stated as generalizations (Borders & Leddick, 1987; Clark & Paivio, 1989; Fowler & Longabaugh, 1975; Mager, 1972; Tomm & Sanders, 1983). For example, should the supervisor observe that in performing marital therapy the therapist "needs to improve his response to clients' emotional expressions," then the supervisor might write this statement at the top of a page as a goal for supervision. Writing down this statement of the goal is the first step in Mager's (1972) goal analysis. However, this statement appears too vague and general for the therapist to use to change his or her behavior. It would not be of much help to the therapist in learning how to handle affect in the session and it would not help the supervisor determine if the therapist was making progress on achieving the goal or had achieved the goal.

The supervisor then goes to step two, making a list of specific acts the therapist should perform to achieve the goal. The supervisor's list might look something like this:

- Reflect the feelings expressed by either spouse.
- Comment on the impact the expression of feeling is having on the therapist by using "I" messages.
- Ask the partner to reflect the spouse's feeling.
- Ask the person expressing the feeling to clarify or restate the feeling to the spouse by using an "I" message.
- Ask the spouse to comment on the other's expression of feeling using "I" messages.
- Stop being critical of family members' expressions of anger and hostile affect.
- Say something about the clients' affective interaction.

If the supervisor feels that this list about covers the responses the therapist would make in therapy sessions if she or he were to achieve the goal, the supervisor should move on to Mager's (1972) third step, editing the list. The purpose of the editing step is to remove any duplicate items, and to determine if any items are too vague, general, or abstract. For instance in looking over the list, the supervisor will note that the last item, "Say something about the clients' affective interaction," is repeating points already made and that this item could be eliminated.

The supervisor might also note that the next to last item, "Stop being critical of family members' expressions of anger and hostile affect," seems different from the other items and may need to be removed or rewritten. The "stop being critical" item is different in that it is asking the spouse to *stop* doing something rather than asking the spouse to *do* something. It is also different in that it focuses specifically on anger and hostility. Perhaps it could be made into a new goal such as, "Help the therapist learn alternate ways to deal with negative affect expressed among family members." It would then be treated just as other goals are treated, that is a list of actions would be made, edited, tested, and presented as a goal.

After the list has been edited the supervisor goes to the fourth step, testing the list by asking, "If the therapist did all these things, would he or she have achieved the goal as stated?" If the answer is "yes," then the supervisor has completed the goal statement and is ready to establish the action steps for the goal. The supervisor might note that the responses listed do not cover all of the affective issues implied in the first statement. Therefore, additional goal statements should be written to handle client expressions of "low or depressed mood" and "anger and hostile affect" in order to fulfill the original abstract goal. Client affective responses between marital couples that are expressions of "low mood or depression," and "anger or hostility" require responses on the part of the therapist that differ from the responses required for affect that falls in the normal range.

The original goal statement was, "The therapist needs to improve his responses to clients' emotional expressions." The refined goal might be similar to this:

> Each time the clients make an affect laden statement or other-wise express an emotion in the session, the therapist will iden-tify the affect statement or expression and its impact upon him, and then determine if the affect statement is an expression of "low mood or depression," "anger or hostility," or an expres-sion of affect within the normal range. If the affect being ex-pressed is within the normal range then the therapist will do one of the following:
>
> - Reflect the feelings expressed by either spouse.
> - Comment on the impact the expression of feeling is having on the therapist by using "I" messages.
> - Ask the partner to reflect the spouse's feeling.
> - Ask the person expressing the feeling to clarify or restate the feeling to the spouse by using an "I" message.
> - Ask the spouse to comment on the other's expression of feeling using "I" messages.
>
> If the clients' affective statements fall within the definition of "low or depressed mood," or "anger and hostility," then the therapist will refer to the responses for that class of affective behavior.

Establishing action steps. Supervision goals should include the action steps needed for the therapist to achieve the desired outcomes. Action steps, like goal statements, should be clear, specific, and observable. For example, if the therapist's goal is to reduce her or his blaming statements and replace them with reframed statements, then the action statement might be something like, "Each time the clients make a statement that could be followed by a critical or blaming statement by me, I will attempt to reframe the statement into one of care and concern." "Critical comments" and "care and concerned comments" could be further defined into clear, specific, and observable statements acceptable to both supervisor and therapist.

Long-term goals, such as achieving an integrated personal theory of therapy, may require a series of intermediate steps. For example, the broad steps toward acquiring an integrated personal theory appear to be to first establish a basic theoretical model from which to work. Second, to learn to apply that model with a variety of classes of clients with a variety of classes of problems. Third, learn to recognize when the basic model does not work well with certain classes of clients and with some classes of problems. Fourth, when the basic model does not appear to work well, explore other models and their techniques that appear relevant for the clients and the problems that are not resolved by the basic model. Finally, integrate these additional models and techniques into a personal, integrated model and be able to describe to others one's own rationale for selecting one technique over another for these particular clients with this specific set of problems. This process continues throughout supervision until the therapist has developed a personal integrated working model of therapy.

One job for the therapist and supervisor may be to discover where the therapist is located on this journey toward an integrated personal model and to determine what the next achievable steps might be. For a beginning therapist, the first steps might be to establish a basic theoretical model. Beyond that step the therapist may need to learn to apply that model with a variety of clients and with a range of problems. More advanced therapists may need to begin to learn additional models. This will mean giving up the notion that the basic model they have adopted can do everything. Advanced therapists will need to determine how the different models relate to each other in a coherent integrated way which they may then apply with efficiency and proficiency.

Even these steps must then be broken down into more achievable steps. For example, learning to apply a model may require learning to observe and identify specific events in clients' patterns of communication. In learning to do family therapy, for instance, can the therapist identify patterns of excessive use of blaming; excessive "mind reading" or "checking out with a powerful member of the family before speaking;" and so on? If the therapist is not able to observe and identify these and similar patterns, the therapist and supervisor may establish a goal to learn to do so, first by observing them on a video tape and labeling them out loud as they occur. Later the therapist may practice observing the clients' communication patterns in an actual session where she or he is taking a client history, and then make appropriate comments about the patterns, in session. As the therapist makes these gains, the supervisor will be evaluating the progress and supplying appropriate feedback.

Evaluating goal achievement. The final step in goal setting is to identify ways to evaluate the outcome. In the example provided, the therapist and supervisor might agree to set the criterion for success as identifying the specified client communication patterns 80 percent of the time in the next three sessions. As the therapist achieves success with this goal, his or her performance should prove reinforcing to both therapist and supervisor. Motivation should be high and they would then be ready to move on to the next supervision goal.

Therapist's Goals and Supervisor's Goals

The therapist's supervision goals and the supervisor's goals for the therapist are almost certain to differ. Discrepancies occur between therapists' and supervisors' goals for supervision for several reasons. First, therapists' perceptions of their goals are likely to vary according to their histories of experience with therapy and supervision. Second, therapists may be unaware of goals that may be required by the profession through accreditation requirements, by the state through licensing requirements, or by the training institution's administrative requirements. Third, supervisors, even within the same training institution, will vary in their expectations for therapist performance.

Goal discrepancies due to therapists' experience histories. As suggested earlier, therapists will tend to perceive their goals in supervision according to their previous history with therapy and supervision. Beginning therapists generally want support and specific technical help for their cases (McNeill et al., 1985; Reising & Daniels, 1983; Stoltenberg & Delworth, 1987; Worthington & Roehlke, 1979). Therefore, their goals will be to get support and approval from their supervisor and to find solutions for their immediate therapy problems. Supervisors tend to respond with support and with technical help (Miars et al., 1983; Worthington, 1984a). However, supervisors must develop strategies and tactics to help the therapist learn to use empirical findings and theory to deal with classes of problems, rather than finding a technique to fix a specific problem (Borders & Leddick, 1987; Stoltenberg & Delworth, 1987; Holloway & Wolleat, 1981). This difference in focus will lead supervisors and beginning therapists to have different goals for supervision. The result may be conflict and deterioration of the supervisor-therapist relationship unless these issues are made clear as part of the supervision goals and negotiated solutions are developed for the supervision plan.

The supervisor's attempts to get intermediate therapists to leave their familiar theories and methods and to try out new theories and techniques may also lead to discrepancies between the therapist's goals and those of the supervisor (Stoltenberg & Delworth, 1987). Intermediate level therapists sometimes struggle with the inadequacies of their preferred theoretical position and begin to search about for other models that will help them solve their clinical problems. However, intermediate therapists often attempt to continue to use the methods and techniques that have become familiar, even when those methods no longer work to solve the clinical problems confronting them (Stoltenberg & Delworth, 1987). Supervisors must encourage therapists to try out new theories, techniques, and methods while helping them to struggle with their confusion and frustration in letting go of methods that they had come to believe would work with everyone, all of the time.

More advanced therapists, who have mastered a wide range of theoretical models and techniques, may be in danger of settling for an unexamined eclecticism (Brabeck & Welfel, 1985). They have developed a number of ways to resolve clinical issues and carry on the practice of therapy. However, often they are unable to articulate why they have selected a particular method or technique. They apply what feels correct to them, but may be unable to specify the principles that apply. It is up to the supervisor to push the therapist to clarify and specify his or her personal model of therapy and to formulate it into an integrated and coherent whole (Stoltenberg & Delworth, 1987). When therapists can specify the principle that applies with specific types of clients with specific sets of problems, then the principles can perhaps be generalized to other similar clients and problems. The therapist's goal to do what feels right and the supervisor's goal to get the therapist to apply a principle may be seen as a supervision goal discrepancy.

Supervisors and therapists almost universally have a problem with paradigm clash. It has been suggested that conflicts over therapy models are among the more difficult problems encountered in supervision (Moskowitz & Rupert, 1983). Learning a new theory is generally much more difficult than most people anticipate. Therefore, it is important to identify this and any other therapist history issues during the goal-setting stage of supervision. Supervisor and therapist can then set goals to negotiate how they will work to resolve these issues over the course of supervision.

Other areas of discrepancy between supervisors and therapists occur around professionally, legally, and institutionally imposed goals. An additional source of goal discrepancies may arise due to the personal orientation of the supervisor. The externally imposed issues will be discussed next.

Goal discrepancies due to externally imposed goals. Many professional, legal, and institutional goals will be imposed upon the supervisor and therapist. These externally imposed goals may be known to the supervisor, but not to the therapist.

The goals established by the professional organizations are determined by the various professional organizations' ethical codes and accreditation requirements. The goals established by the state are determined by the laws enacted by legislative bodies. Additional legal issues result from precedent-setting cases such as the Tarasoff case (Wilson, 1981). Ethical standards and legal precedents tend to establish practices that come to be recognized as standards of practice. Supervisors are responsible for seeing to it that their trainees meet or exceed these standards of therapy performance.

The goals established by training institutions are the institution's stated and unstated policies. Such policies may determine which theory or theories will be taught within that setting, the facilities that will be made available, and the supervision methods that will be accepted. All of the professionally, legally, and institutionally imposed goals must be taken into account by the supervisor and therapist as they work together to establish the supervision goals. In addition, the supervisor's personal expectations must also be made into explicit supervision goals.

Goal discrepancies due to the supervisor's expectations. Inasmuch as the supervisor's personal expectations for the therapist in supervision differ from those of the therapist, there will be potential for difficulties in the supervisor-therapist relationship. Therefore, the supervisor's personal expectations for the supervision process should be made as explicit as possible. For example, the supervisor's personal preferences for a therapy theory, for specific therapeutic techniques, and for specific methods of doing supervision should be clearly stated prior to beginning supervision. If both the supervisor and therapist can clearly state their goals, differences can more easily be identified and acceptable compromises negotiated prior to writing out the final supervision plan.

One of the major tasks in supervision is helping therapists to identify and state their goals for supervision. We turn next to some procedures supervisors can use to help therapists clarify their supervision goals.

Helping Therapists Establish Goals for Supervision

In the discussion above the impact of the therapist's history on the supervision goals was described. In addition to specific goals related to learning to do therapy, the therapist may bring along other goals.

Greenberg (1980) and others (Liddle, Davidson, & Barrett, 1988; Loganbill, Hardy, & Delworth, 1982; Stoltenberg & Delworth, 1987) have described several goals that therapists may have when they enter supervision. Although the therapist's fundamental goal in supervision may be to learn a specific skill or technique of therapy, he or she may also be seeking to evaluate therapy as a career, searching for support and reinforcement, looking for answers to personal problems, seeking personal growth and development, or attempting to evaluate and/or validate a specific theoretical model. Therefore, failure of the supervisor to help the therapist to clarify and specify his or her expectations, attitudes, and goals related to supervision may lead to miscommunication and frustration for both the therapist and the supervisor.

Clarifying the therapist's expectations and attitudes. It seems likely that the therapist's expectations about the changes she or he will be expected to make in supervision may influence the course of supervision (Schwartz, 1988). Hirsch and Stone (1982) have demonstrated in a supervision analogue study that positive trainee attitudes toward a therapy technique resulted in significantly higher quality responses with that technique. It would be nice if therapists could always be matched to supervisors who are going to supervise them in techniques toward which they are positively disposed. However, attempts to match therapists with supervisors have met with mixed results (Cherniss & Egnatios, 1977).

Because it is not always possible or even desirable to match therapists and supervisors, what can be done to help them overcome some of the problems of discrepant goals? As already mentioned, one thing that supervisors can do to help is to clarify and specify the goals for supervision at all levels, that is, the therapist's goals, the externally imposed goals, and the supervisor's personal expectations. Wherever possible, the discrepancies should be clarified and negotiated compromises worked out using good communication procedures and the basic problem solving skills described in Figure 3.1. (see pp. 43–45).

Where compromise is not possible—for example, where only one theory of treatment will be acceptable in a given supervision setting or a given block of training time, such as a semester; or where some treatment appears to be the clear treatment of choice for a specific problem—then efforts should be made by the supervisor to provide ample motivation for the behavior the therapist is expected to perform.

From our analysis of motivation in Chapter 3, increasing therapist motivation for doing therapy appears to be largely a function of increasing reinforcement and reducing punishment. Forging a working relationship is primarily a method of establishing a nonpunishing environment. Showing the therapist respect, care, and empathy makes it possible for the therapist to try out therapeutic behaviors with less fear of punishment. Removing competition from the supervision group also serves to reduce punishment from supervision. Searching for therapist strengths and pointing up successes may serve as reinforcement. Setting realistic goals with clear and specific markers of progress increases the potential for reinforcement and reduces the potential for punishment.

Supervisor's goals. The primary goal of supervision is to help therapists become more expert in their therapy performance. Under this goal will be the more specific goals established by the therapist and supervisor together in consultation. These specific goals might include learning the basic theoretical components of the therapy model to be used, learning what to observe and how to observe it, learning how to conceptualize the cases, learning how to formulate a treatment plan, learning how to deliver a specific form of treatment, and learning how to evaluate progress. Even more specifically, the goals may be to learn how to teach clients to be assertive (Lange & Jakubowski, 1976), how to reframe (Fisch, 1988; Haas, Alexander, & Mas, 1988), how to do a specific initial interview, such as Watzlawick's structured family interview (1966), how to help a family member differentiate from his or her family of origin (Papero, 1988), and so on.

The supervisor may also look to research and supervision theory to establish goals for supervision. According to Kniskern and Gurman

(1988) there are three sets of variables related to therapists' behavior in therapy: (1) experience level, (2) structuring skills, and (3) relationship skills. They also argue that only the latter two are teachable. However, the goal of supervision as presented here is to make the therapist into an expert or experienced therapist. To accomplish this the supervisor must determine what experienced therapists do in clinical sessions that is different from what inexperienced therapists do. Supervisors can then present supervision goals that consist of doing those things that experienced therapists do. In this way supervisors will be "teaching" experience. As Kniskern and Gurman (1988) point out, experienced therapists use relationship skills to establish a working relationship with each family member. Experienced therapists use structuring skills to establish good therapeutic practices in their sessions. And according to Pinsof (1979), experienced family therapists use a wider variety of interventions and are more active in sessions than are beginning therapists. Therefore, these skills should be included in the supervision goals, if they are not already a part of the therapist's repertoire.

The developmental theory of supervision (Stoltenberg & Delworth, 1987) suggests a number of goals for supervision that the supervisor may wish to consider while establishing the supervision plan. These authors suggest that the supervisor consider three structural goals: (1) therapist awareness of the affect occurring in the session in himself or herself and the affect being expressed by the clients; (2) the therapist's motivation for therapy and supervision, as discussed in Chapter 3; and (3) the degree of autonomy the therapist is able to exercise in conducting therapy. In addition, Stoltenberg and Delworth (1987) suggest that the supervisor consider these three structures as they occur in a number of therapy domains. Specifically, the therapy domains include: intervention skills; assessment skills; client conceptualization skills; awareness of individual differences such as gender, ethnic, and cultural differences; theoretical orientation; treatment goals and plans; and professional ethics.

The Task-Oriented Model may also serve as the basis for overcoming therapist and supervisor discrepancies in supervision goals. In the process of developing the therapist's data base, the supervisor may come to recognize the therapist's ability to identify the tasks the client should be engaged in at any point in the therapy (see Figure 2.1, Level 1) and the therapist's ability to match the client tasks with appropriate therapist tasks (see Figure 2.1, Level 2). Based upon the supervisor's understanding of the therapist's ability to perceive, conceptualize, and execute appropriate action relative to the tasks described by the Task-Oriented Model, the supervisor can then move to establish goals to build and/or maintain those task related skills. For example, the supervisor may set forth a goal of helping the therapist determine which task is appropriate for these clients at this time, or the supervisor may establish a goal of helping the therapist use the tasks identified by the Task-Oriented Model to create a bridge from the practice of using a single approach to accomplish a task to the practice of identifying and using a number of theories and techniques to accomplish that task.

SUMMARY

The supervisor has a vast array of goals that may be specified for any one training block. Before establishing the goals for this block, the supervisor may wish to survey the field briefly. The supervisor should list the goals of the therapist, the goals of the training institution, the professional and legal goals, and the goals expected by the supervisor. Since the number of goals an individual can work on at any one time is relatively limited, it is important that the supervisor selects from the list of goals the three to five most important goals. This abbreviated list should be discussed with the therapist and a limited number of mutually agreeable goals should be selected for the supervision plan during this block of training time.

Once the goals have been established with the therapist, the supervisor is ready to specify the procedures that will be used to observe the therapist's performance with clients in therapy sessions.

CHAPTER 5

Developing the Supervision Plan

INTRODUCTION

Once the supervisor and therapist have developed a working relationship, established the therapist data base, and have settled on a set of mutually acceptable goals for supervision, the supervisor must consider how best to observe the therapist's treatment delivery and the impact of the therapist's treatment on the clients. In addition, the supervisor must decide how to observe the therapist's perceptions of his or her treatment delivery and the therapist's perceptions of the treatment impact on the clients. The supervisor must also determine how the therapist will be assessed and evaluated over the course of the supervision sessions. Finally, the supervisor brings all this information together into the initial written supervision plan. The initial supervision plan may be revised when the therapist achieves some of the supervision goals or under other circumstances such as the lack of clients.

The supervision plan should be a written plan that specifies requirements for successful completion of the supervision. The plan generally contains eight basic sections:

1. the supervisor's preparation for supervision;
2. the conditions and expectations for supervision;
3. the supervisor's understanding of the therapist's preparation for therapy;
4. the goals to be achieved in this supervision block;

5. the procedures the supervisor will use to observe the therapist delivering clinical treatment and the impact of the treatment on the clients;
6. the procedures the supervisor will employ to determine the therapist's clinical reasoning and decision making;
7. the procedures the supervisor will use to evaluate the therapist's progress;
8. the procedures the supervisor will use to intervene to help the therapist achieve the supervision goals.

Each of the sections of the supervision plan will be reviewed briefly to show how they pertain to the overall plan.

The Eight Sections of the Supervision Plan
1. *Supervisor's preparation.* The supervision plan should contain a brief description of the supervisor's preparation for supervision which may be shared with prospective trainees (see Chapter 2). This description may include information such as the supervisor's education, the supervisor's preferred mode of performing therapy, and the supervisor's model of supervision. This information may appear in a handout or brochure that is issued to prospective supervisees before they enter supervision or upon entering supervision.
2. *Conditions and expectations.* The supervision plan should provide the trainee with information about the conditions and expectations for supervision that are imposed by the profession, the state, and the training institutions (see Chapter 3). This section of the supervision plan should include details about the following:

   • the model of therapy to be taught in this training block,
   • specific techniques and treatment programs to be learned,
   • numbers and types of clients to be expected and what will happen if there are not enough clients,
   • expectations for numbers and duration of supervision meetings,
   • what to do in emergencies,
   • expectations about the collection of fees,
   • the nature and frequency of therapist-trainee evaluations,
   • the nature and frequency of site visits.

Issues related to the confidentiality of supervisor and therapist communications should also be shared in this section of the supervision plan as should grievance procedures that may be used when necessary. This section of the supervision plan, as in the case of section 1, may be part of a handout that is distributed to prospective supervisees prior to beginning supervision.

3. *Therapist's preparation.* The information from the supervisor's therapist data base (see Chapter 3) is contained in this section of the plan. The information is gathered by the supervisor from the therapist in collaboration with the therapist. The description and rationale of the procedures used to create the therapist data base should be included in the supervision plan. The procedures themselves, and the rationale behind them, should be described to the therapist prior to actually gathering the data. This section of the supervision plan concerns the therapist's preparation to do therapy with the sorts of problems presented by the types of clients the therapist will be seeing in this agency and in this training block. The supervisor should attempt to describe the therapist's strengths in applying treatment in the clinical setting as concretely as possible. Areas of therapist deficiency should also be noted specifically and clearly.

4. *Supervision goals.* The supervisor and the therapist should collaborate to establish supervision goals for this training period (see Chapter 4). The goals should be based upon the conditions and expectations for supervision and the therapist's preparation for therapy as set forth in the second and third sections. That is, there should be a logical connection between the goals, the conditions and expectations, and the therapist's preparation. In addition, the goals should clearly state the specific steps the therapist must take to accomplish the goals.

5. *Supervisor's observation of treatment delivery.* The supervisor should select the procedures to be used to observe the therapist's delivery of treatment and specify those procedures in the supervision plan. The procedures used to select the observation methods to be employed are discussed later in this chapter, and the process of observation is discussed in Chapter 6. The supervisor should select the observation procedures based upon: the trainee's skill level, the availability of technical equipment, the degree of observational fidelity needed, the potential need to intervene in the therapist's treatment, and the need for timely interviews to determine the therapist's observations of and affective responses to the

session. The observation methods and procedures should be described as well as the rationale for selecting them.

The supervision plan should also include any special preparation for supervision that will be required of the therapist. For example, if the therapist will be required to prepare video tapes in a particular way for viewing in the supervision sessions, the appropriate instructions should be part of the supervision plan.

6. *Determining the therapist's clinical reasoning.* The supervision plan should clearly state the procedures the supervisor will use to determine the therapist's clinical reasoning and decision making (see Chapter 7). The supervisor's expectations and procedures also should be clarified. The rationale for these procedures should be specified. As these procedures will generally take the form of an interview, any special preparation that the therapist will be required to make prior to the interview should be stated in this section of the supervision plan. For example, the therapist might be instructed to be prepared to respond to a list of questions such as those outlined in Figure 5.1 or those found in Chapter 3 (see Figure 3.1).

7. *Evaluating therapist progress.* The supervision plan should spell out for the therapist the evaluation procedures that will apply for this supervision block. Evaluation of supervision, to be effective, may need to take place on all three levels of the Task-Oriented Model—the client level, the therapist level, and the supervisor level (see Figure 2.1). Therefore, the supervision plan should specify the numbers and types of assessments that will be required, who will make the assessments, and when the assessments will be made.

8. *Procedures for intervening by the supervisor.* The supervision plan should include a description of the procedures the supervisor will use to intervene with the therapist to provide corrective feedback and to help the therapist reach the supervision goals (Chapter 7). Intervention procedures may be restricted by the form of observation selected. For example, live supervision provides the opportunity for a wide range of direct interventions, such as phoning in instructions, and knocking on the door and inviting the therapist to come behind the one-way screen. Self-report case note sessions, on the other hand, generally restrict the supervisor to interventions such as modeling, role play, and directives to be executed in later sessions. Whatever methods are to be employed should be described for the therapist in the supervision plan.

The following questions may be used by a supervisor before, during, or following a therapy session to determine the therapist's clinical reasoning.

Task Selection
- Ask what task* is appropriate for these clients at this time.
- Ask what task the therapist is engaged in with these clients at this time.
- Ask yourself what task the supervisor should be engaged in at this time.
- Ask what theory the therapist is applying to this task.
- Ask what principles from that theory apply to this task.
- Ask what variables the theory would suggest are influencing behavior, affect, and cognitions related to this task.
- Pick a counter example for an insufficient variable.
- Pick a counter example for an unnecessary variable.
- Pick an example with the same variables.

Ask for Variables
- Ask for antecedent variables.
- Ask for intermediate variables.
- Ask for subsequent variables.
- Ask for consequent variables.
- Ask how a response or pattern depends upon a given variable.

Prediction
- Ask for a prediction about a particular task.

Confrontation
- Pose a misleading question.
- Form a general rule for an insufficient variable.
- Form a general rule for an unnecessary variable.

Probe Clinical Reasoning Strategy and Hypothesis Testing
- Request a test of a hypothesis about a variable.
- Ask what are the relevant variables to consider.
- Test for consistency of theory, principles, or variables with a given hypothesis.

Inform Trainee
- Inform trainee of the correct task(s) or relationship(s).
- Point out necessary variables.
- Point out sufficient variables.

Insufficient Variables
- Form a general rule for an insufficient variable.
- Pick a counter example for an insufficient variable.
- Probe for a necessary variable.
- Point out a necessary variable.
- Probe for similarities between two tasks, events, patterns, or cases.

(continued)

Figure 5.1. Basic Questioning Pattern to Determine Clinical Reasoning

Unnecessary Variables
- Form a general rule for an unnecessary variable.
- Pick a counter example for an unnecessary variable.
- Probe for a sufficient variable.
- Point out a sufficient variable.
- Probe for similarities between two tasks, events, patterns, or cases.

Information Collection
- Question a prediction or a hypothesis or a treatment plan made without enough information.
- Point out an inconsistent prediction.
- Ask for consideration of a possible outcome value.
- Ask for consideration of a relevant variable.
- Ask about the most efficient ways to collect the needed information.

Forming Hypotheses
- Ask for antecedent variables.
- Ask for intermediate variables.
- Ask for subsequent variables.
- Ask for consequent variables.
- Form a general rule for an insufficient variable.
- Form a general rule for an unnecessary variable.
- Pick a counter example for an insufficient variable.
- Pick a counter example for an unnecessary variable.
- Probe for a necessary variable.
- Probe for a sufficient variable.
- Probe for similarities between two tasks, events, patterns, or cases.
- Probe for differences between two tasks, events, patterns, or cases.

---

*Tasks refer to the tasks outline in the Task–Oriented Model (see Figure 2.1).
(Adapted from Albert L. Stevens and Allan Collins [1977]. The goal structure of a Socratic tutor. *Proceedings of the Association for Computing Machinery Annual Conference*, 256–263. Copyright 1977 by IEEE Publishing Services.)

The supervision plan consists of the eight sections described. All eight sections are important elements of the supervision plan, but they may appear separately as needed. For example, Sections 1 and 2 may be presented to the therapist before she or he enters supervision or in the first supervision session.

The remainder of this chapter sets forth a description of the observation procedures that may be available to the supervisor. It also presents a review of some of the assessment and evaluation procedures from which the supervisor may select for evaluating the therapist's progress and the outcome of the supervision block.

SELECTING THE OBSERVATION PROCEDURES

One of the most important functions performed by the supervisor is assumed to be the establishment of procedures to observe the therapist's skill in delivering treatment. Supervisors, in order to perform their supervisory functions, must establish effective and efficient ways to observe the therapist's in-session clinical behaviors. The supervisor may decide how the therapist will be observed either unilaterally or in conjunction with the therapist. In addition, the decision is based, in part, upon the physical facilities and equipment available (Birchler, 1975; Matarazzo, 1978).

Generally, four methods to determine therapists' performance in therapy may be used. Three of these methods are observational methods and the fourth is a self-report method. The three observational methods are: (1) "live" observation in which the supervisor observes the session as it is occurring, either through a one-way mirror or by means of closed circuit TV* (Berger & Dammann, 1982; Cornwell & Pearson, 1981; Mendelsohn & Ferber, 1972; Montalvo, 1973; Rickert & Turner, 1978; Schwartz, Liddle, & Breunlin, 1988); (2) postsession observation by means of video or audio tape (Breunlin et al., 1988; Kramer & Reitz, 1980); and (3) Co-therapy with the supervisor participating in the therapy session to observe the therapist's performance. The fourth method used to determine the therapist's performance is postsession presentation of the case notes self-reported by the therapist.

Each of the methods of determining therapist performance has advantages and disadvantages. For example, the fidelity of the supervisor's information concerning the events that occur in the therapist's clinical sessions is perhaps greatest for co-therapy and live supervision and least when the therapist presents the case from his or her notes. The fidelity of the session refers to the degree of accuracy and exactness of the information the supervisor has about the session. Fidelity is greater the more the supervisor is directly exposed to the actual session variables, such as the press of time and the expression of affect by both clients and therapist through subtle body movements, voice tones, and so on (Birchler, 1975; Mead & Crane, 1978). Therefore, fidelity is greater the closer the observation method is to actual therapy.

Using live observation. In addition to providing the supervisor with relatively high fidelity for session variables, observation of therapist performance in live sessions has the advantage that the supervisor can intervene with the therapist while the therapist is in the act of performing therapy (Birchler, 1975). The supervisor can intervene, if

---

*Live supervision has also been conducted without one-way screens or closed circuit TV; for example, see Smith and Kingston (1980).

deemed appropriate, by phoning in messages, by knocking on the door and inviting the therapist to step out, or by walking into the session. The potential for the supervisor to intervene directly in the session is especially helpful when the therapist lacks experience in doing therapy or in using a specific technique or treatment program.

One of the disadvantages of live supervision as a method of observing the therapist's performance is that it requires the supervisor to be physically present when the interview is occurring (Birchler, 1975). Therefore, live observation may be more time-consuming than some other forms of supervision. The time required for live supervision often includes time for the presession interview, the time of the session itself, and the time required for a postsession debriefing (Heath, 1983).

The act of intervening, though considered an advantage by some, may be seen as a disadvantage by others. There are still questions in the minds of some therapists about the therapeutic and ethical implications of the supervisor intervening during the actual session. One of the questions centers on the supervisor doing therapy through the trainee (Schwartz, Liddle, & Breunlin, 1988). Others might question the ethics of the supervisor, a stranger in many ways, breaking into the therapist–client system and thereby creating a new system. Ultimately, whether these advantages and disadvantages of live supervision turn out to be beneficial or harmful in therapy will need to be determined by empirical study.

Upon considering the advantages and disadvantages of live supervision, it appears that live supervision may be most appropriate for beginning and intermediate therapists or for therapists who are implementing a technique that is entirely new for them. The cost in supervision time may be justified with beginning therapists who have a high potential for misdiagnosing cases (Spitzer et al., 1982) or otherwise doing harm to the clients. The cost may also be justified as an evaluation procedure for determining therapists' skills and their progress toward becoming competent, expert therapists.

Using taped observations. Observations by video or audio tape also have advantages and disadvantages (Birchler, 1975; Breunlin, Karrer, McGuire, & Cimmarusti, 1988). One of the advantages of observing the session by tape is that the supervisor may observe the tape at her or his convenience. Another advantage is that the supervisor may stop the tape for discussion at important points without concern for the therapeutic and ethical questions about the impact of breaking into the ongoing session. Yet another advantage of taped sessions is that they can be used for training, education, and research. Both the clients and the therapist must give their permission for the tape to be used for research purposes.

Among the disadvantages of taped sessions is loss of fidelity as compared with live supervision. The lack of opportunity to intervene while the session is in progress is another disadvantage. If the supervisor observes a major error and immediate treatment is needed, either the therapist or the supervisor must act to contact the clients to correct the error. If immediate treatment is not needed but correction is still called for, the therapist must take time in the next session to rectify the problem. In addition, extra time must be allotted for the supervisor or therapist to prepare the tapes for the supervision session (Breunlin et al., 1988). However, the process of reviewing tapes to pick out examples of specific forms of therapist behavior for later review in supervision can be a very good learning experience for the beginning or intermediate therapist.

When immediate intervention of the supervisor may be needed, the use of video or audio tape supervision may be contraindicated. On the other hand, with intermediate and advanced therapists the lack of opportunity to intervene in the ongoing sessions may be an advantage. Therapists who will be observed on tape may feel more independent and more responsible for the case than those who are observed live (Miars et al., 1983; Reising & Daniels, 1983). As one of the goals of supervision is to help therapists become more independent, it follows that as beginning therapists gain more competence the supervisor may wish to move them from live supervision to video or audio tape.

Using case notes. Use of case note presentations to determine the therapist's ability to deliver treatment and to assess the impact of therapy on the clients also has advantages and disadvantages. One of the advantages of case note presentation is that it requires little or no technical equipment. Another advantage is that it requires little additional time from either the supervisor or the therapist. Perhaps the greatest advantage of the case note method may come with more advanced therapists in that it may give the trainee a stronger sense of independence and responsibility for the welfare of the clients than either live supervision or tape playback methods (Miars et al., 1983; Reising & Daniels, 1983).

The case note presentation method of determining the therapist's performance in therapy suffers from several major disadvantages. First, case note presentations offer the least fidelity between the events in the session and the information available to the supervisor. Second, unlike the other methods, case note presentation offers no opportunity for the supervisor to observe and experience the session variables. Third, the supervisor is not able to intervene in the ongoing sessions, but must recommend action for later, as with the taped sessions.

Lack of fidelity is a major disadvantage of this method of determining therapist performance because case note presentations suffer from all the hazards of other self-report methods (Hess, 1980). Case notes are *ex post facto,* they are subject to editing, and they are subject to problems of recall. For example, Spitzer et al. (1982) report that when therapists present their diagnosis of the clients' problems to the supervisor in case presentations, if the therapist's diagnosis of the case is in error, the supervisor's diagnosis is likely to be in error too. The information that the therapist may have overlooked cannot be known to the supervisor from case note presentations.

Considering the advantages and disadvantages of the case note presentation method one might conclude that it may be best used only with advanced therapists. When the supervisor wishes to signal that the therapist is capable of independent therapy, he or she may switch from live or tape playback methods of supervision to case note presentations. The case note method seems contraindicated for beginning and intermediate therapists whenever adequate technical assistance is available to support live supervision or taped sessions. However, in a study by Fenell, Hovestadt, and Harvey (1986) neither the use of live supervision or case note presentations seemed to directly influence the therapists' scores on a family therapist rating scale. Further research in this area is needed as the Fenell et al. (1986) study has a number of weaknesses that suggest that the results should be considered very tentative.

Using co-therapy. The advantage in using co-therapy as a method of observing the therapist's ability to deliver treatment is that the supervisor, acting as co-therapist, is present in the actual treatment room (Abroms, 1977). Fidelity is almost one to one. The ethical and therapeutic issues related to supervisor interventions that are a concern in live supervision, such as phoning in or walking into an ongoing session, are eliminated. However, a number of disadvantages are associated with using co-therapy for observations and supervision.

One of the major disadvantages of using co-therapy occurs with beginning and intermediate trainees. When an experienced supervisor sits in with a very inexperienced therapist, the supervisor often finds it difficult or even impossible not to take the lead in the session (Abroms, 1977). Clients and beginnning therapists look to the senior member for leadership. The welfare of the clients often seems to demand that the more experienced therapist take action. The result is that co-therapy does not provide an opportunity to observe and evaluate the trainee, but rather co-therapy often becomes an occasion for the supervisor to model therapy (Abroms, 1977; Thompson & Blocher, 1979). For certain teaching purposes modeling is excellent, but co-therapy does not appear to be a useful method to observe and supervise therapist performance.

Even when the therapist is experienced enough to take the lead in a co-therapy session, the supervisor may still find it difficult to use the session for observation. When the supervisor does not take the lead in the session, but mainly observes the therapist's performance, the supervisor may appear to the other participants as just that, an observer rather than a participant. The effect of being observed by a person in the same room will undoubtedly influence the course of the therapy in some way. This will make it difficult for the supervisor to determine if any changes in the clients' behaviors were due to the therapist's treatment or due to the presence of the supervisor-observer. Whether this form of observation is more intrusive than being watched through the one-way mirror or being recorded on video tape is an empirical question.

Other objections to co-therapy as a supervision method are that it takes additional time and that it denies the therapist the experience of taking responsibility for the case (Abroms, 1977). Both co-therapy and live supervision require the actual presence of the supervisor during the session, and then additional time outside of the session must be devoted to supervision. Therefore, co-therapy and live supervision do require more of the supervisor's time than supervision by tape or case note review.

Abroms (1977) agrees that co-therapy is shared responsibility for the case but suggests that this is useful in as much as it teaches therapists to confer with others about their cases. Abroms points out that many therapists working solo have trouble going to a trusted colleague when they are having difficulty, perhaps because they have never had the experience of sharing the case with another in co-therapy.

In considering the pros and cons of co-therapy we must also address its utility for training therapists for practice. Generally, the economics of practice rule out opportunities for co-therapy in the working environment. Therefore, in training, co-therapy should be used sparingly—if at all—as it is preparing therapists for behavior which will only rarely be used in clinical practice in the field.

Selecting an Observation Method

The method the supervisor selects to observe the therapist's skills in delivering therapy seems to be based upon several factors: (1) availability of one-way screens, television, and so on; (2) the degree of fidelity needed for observation and the need to intervene in the ongoing session; (3) the need for timeliness of the supervisor's interview of the therapist about the therapist's observations; and (4) the factor that seems to underlie all three of the above issues, the performance level of the therapists who are in supervision.

Availability of technical equipment. The first factor, as discussed earlier, is the availability of the technical equipment for live or video and audio taped observation of sessions. Availability of technical equipment is a function of administrative decisions concerning aims of the agency, financial support, and so on. If the technical equipment is not available and the nature of the therapists to be supervised requires live or taped supervision, then it is the responsibility of the supervisor to bring this to the attention of the administration.

Need for fidelity and ability to intervene. The second factor, assuming that the necessary equipment is available, is the supervisor's need for fidelity of the session observations and the capability to intervene with the therapist's treatment delivery in a timely fashion. Cotherapy and live supervision provide greater fidelity and more immediate access for intervention. Lowest fidelity and immediate intervention capability are found in the case presentation method. The criteria used by supervisors to select an observation method is not presently clear. A recent study found that the case presentation method is the one most frequently used by marriage and family therapy supervisors, followed by video tapes, audio tapes, live supervision, and cotherapy (Wetchler, Piercy, & Sprenkle, 1989). It appears likely that similar results would be found in the other mental health professions. In the study by Wetchler et al., the method rated most effective by both supervisors and supervisees was use of video playback. The study did not attempt to determine the criteria used by the supervisors for their selection of methods, and further study in this area is needed. Until empirical evidence is available about the usefulness of one approach to supervision over another, the supervisor will need to make this decision based upon his or her best clinical judgment.

Timeliness of the interviews about the therapist's observations. The supervisor needs to interview the therapist about the therapist's observations and affective reactions to the session in order to determine the therapist's clinical reasoning about the case. The issues related to timeliness of the interview are discussed in the section concerning clinical reasoning.

Therapist's performance levels. The fourth factor used by supervisors to select a method to observe how well therapists perform is the therapist's basic skill level. The therapist's basic skill level appears to underlie all of the issues discussed above. It is important for the supervisor to have greater fidelity with less experienced therapists. However, the relationship of method of supervisor observation to therapist skill level has not been empirically tested. It is not known whether beginning therapists will learn to perform better with live supervision and immediate feedback, or whether intermediate therapists will benefit from audio or video observation more than other methods of observation, nor are there good criteria to decide when it is best to begin to turn therapists loose to perform therapy with only self-reported case notes as the method of supervisory observation and monitoring.

SELECTING ASSESSMENT PROCEDURES

As already stated, evaluation of supervision may need to occur on all three levels of the Task-Oriented Model. Not only must assessment occur on all three levels, but for many supervision purposes, observation and assessment must occur on a regular or continuous basis.

Continuous evaluation of supervision is necessary on both the therapist and the client levels. Such evaluation is essential because the processes of supervisory observation, evaluation, and supervisory intervention are almost inseparable (see Chapters 6 and 7). The supervisor must be vigilant in observing and evaluating the therapist's treatment delivery in order to be prepared to deliver corrective feedback to the therapist. Similarly, to determine the effect of the therapist's treatment on the clients, the supervisor must be continuously observing and evaluating the clients' responses. The supervisor's interventions should be based upon his or her observations and evaluations of both the therapist and the clients. The nature of the continuous assessment procedures to be used to evaluate the therapist's behavior should be clearly stated in the supervision plan.

The expectations for continuous measurement of the clients that may be the responsibility of the therapist should also be specified in the supervision plan. It may be that these expectations are stated in the supervision plan whereas specific instruments and methods to be used are left to be negotiated with the therapist when the therapist is assessing the client's problems and goals and developing the treatment plan.

In addition to continuous evaluation of the therapist and the clients, the supervisor will need to make outcome evaluations of the therapist's progress. Periodic evaluations are needed during and at the end of the supervision block (see Chapter 8) as supervisors are often asked to provide therapists and interested others with evaluations of the therapist's progress. Therefore, the supervision plan should inform the therapist of the nature, frequency, and timing of any such periodic evaluations. If the supervisor is working in an agency or institute that is separate from the therapist's educational program, the supervision plan should also detail the procedures that will be used for reporting therapist evaluations to the home unit.

The supervision plan should inform the therapist as completely as possible about the evaluation procedures. The types and methods of ratings to be used should be described and the persons doing the rating should also be specified. The therapist should be informed of the types of evaluation to be used, for example, supervisor ratings, peer ratings, ratings by coders, ratings by site visitors from the therapist's home institution, self-report ratings, and/or ratings by the clients. The rating methods should also be spelled out. The supervision plan should state whether the supervisor will evaluate the therapist using subjective ratings, specific inventories or scales, self-report questionnaires, and so on. If specific scales or inventories are to be used, they should be named and a brief description of them supplied.

If the therapist will be required to evaluate the supervisor, these procedures should also be described. The supervisor may wish to consider some form of self-ratings while attending to the evaluation needs for all three levels of the Task–Oriented Model. Although not part of the treatment plan, some form of self-evaluation may be required by the supervisor's supervisor if the supervisor is a supervisor-in-training. In addition the supervisor of the supervisor-in-training may rate the supervisor's performance.

In conclusion, the supervisor's decision concerning the methods to be used to observe the therapist's delivery of treatment and the therapist's responses to the impact of that treatment on the client appear to be based upon the answers to three questions. First, from the therapist data base, "What does this therapist know how to do?" (Chapter 3). Second, from the goals for this supervision block, "What does this therapist need to learn to do?" (Chapter 4). Third, based upon the answers to the previous two questions, "How should the supervisor observe the therapist?" The latter decision appears to depend upon (a) the therapist's skill level, (b) the supervisor's need for timely, high fidelity information about events in the therapy session, (c) the supervisor's need to intervene in the ongoing session, and (d) the need for timely interviews with the therapist to determine the therapist's observations of and affective responses to the session. The supervision plan depends upon the answers to these three questions. As we have seen the various observation methods vary in their usefulness related to these issues.

Presenting the supervision plan. Once the supervisor has prepared the supervision plan, it should be negotiated with the trainee and, if applicable, with the representative from the trainee's home institution. In the latter situation, it may be best if all three can meet together to negotiate the supervision plan. If the supervisor is a supervisor-in-training, then the supervisor-of-the-supervisor may be invited to join this group or the session may be taped for later observation by him or her.

Case assignment. Once the supervisor and therapist have determined the therapist's readiness to do therapy and the goals for supervision have been established, a case may be assigned to the therapist. Where possible the supervisor should assign clients diagnosed as manifesting the problem classes in which the therapist needs to improve her or his treatment delivery skills. The difficulty level of the clients should be equal to the skill level of the therapist or a little beyond, with care being taken to see that the complexity of the case is not overwhelming to a beginning or intermediate level trainee.

CHAPTER 6

Observing Therapists' Behaviors

INTRODUCTION

The supervisor's procedures for observing the therapist's skill in delivering treatment, for observing the impact of the therapist on the clients, and for observing how the therapist reasons clinically about the impact of the treatment on the clients, are not independent procedures. It is difficult, if not impossible, for the supervisor to observe the therapist's skills in delivering treatment without at the same time observing the impact of the therapist's treatment on the clients. Not only would it be difficult to separate these two interdependent processes, but it might be unwise to do so. The supervisor must know the impact of the treatment on the clients to fairly evaluate the therapist. Furthermore, to fairly evaluate the therapist, the supervisor must devise techniques to determine what the therapist is observing and concluding about his or her treatment delivery and its impact. Therefore, the discussion that follows looks first at how supervisors observe therapists delivering treatment and treatment impact, and then at how supervisors determine the therapists' clinical reasoning.

In practice it is difficult to separate observation of the therapist delivering treatment from observations of the impact of treatment on the clients; however, for understanding and teaching it is important to separate the two in our discussions. It is also important to point out that if the supervisor is to succeed in helping the therapist to become a more expert therapist then one task for the supervisor is to help the therapist to become more aware of the impact of his or her treatment on the clients.

This chapter concentrates on the supervisor's tasks of (a) observing therapists delivering treatment, (b) observing the impact of the treatment on clients, and (c) interviewing therapists to determine their clinical reasoning (see Figure 2.1). Chapter 7 describes the supervisor's tasks of evaluating and intervening with therapists, and Chapter 8 examines the supervisory tasks of updating the supervisor's therapist data base and determining the therapist's need for additional supervision.

THE PRINCIPAL TASKS OF THE SUPERVISOR

After completing the tasks associated with developing the supervision plan (Chapters 2, 3, 4, and 5), the supervisor begins the principal tasks of supervision: (1) observing the therapist's delivery of treatment; (2) determining the impact of that treatment on the clients; (3) interviewing the therapist to determine the therapist's clinical reasoning; and (4) helping therapists improve their treatment delivery. The top level goals of supervision are to develop expert therapists and to safeguard the welfare of the clients. The ultimate test of supervision is to produce changes in therapist's clinical behavior that results in positive changes in clients.

Bringing about changes in the therapist's behavior begins with the supervisor observing and interviewing therapists. Only after the supervisor has observed the therapist's skills in delivering treatment and in reasoning about the effects of that treatment will the supervisor be in a position to evaluate the therapist's therapy skills and to intervene to help the therapist become more expert in her or his delivery of therapy.

Some Purposes for Observing Therapists' Behaviors

Observing and interviewing therapists may occur in the therapy consulting room, as in co-therapy, but it is far more likely to take place in viewing rooms watching video tapes or listening to audio tapes and in observation booths watching therapists through one-way mirrors (Wetchler, Piercy, & Sprenkle, 1989). Supervisors appear to spend even more time attempting to determine how therapists deliver treatment by listening to them make case presentations than by observing therapists delivering treatment (Wetchler et al., 1989). And supervisors appear to spend more time attempting to determine how therapists deliver treatment by interviewing therapists in groups than by interviewing them individually (Wetchler et al., 1989). However, at present there appears to be little known about the impact of group supervision on actual treatment delivery (Borders & Leddick, 1987).

The purpose of all this observation and interviewing by supervisors is to help therapists become expert therapists. Supervisors spend time viewing therapists delivering treatment through one-way mirrors, viewing video tapes, listening to audio tapes, and reading case notes to determine the therapists' skills in delivering therapy. Supervisors also spend time observing therapists to prepare to intervene in such a way that the therapist gets better at delivering therapy.

Once they have made their observations, supervisors spend time interviewing therapists for two purposes: to determine the therapist's clinical reasoning about the case and to help therapists improve their delivery of treatment. Supervisors interview therapists for both of these purposes before, during, and after therapy sessions. In this chapter we concentrate on the supervisors' tasks of observation and interviewing about the therapist's clinical reasoning related to the impact of treatment on the clients. The supervisor's tasks of interviewing for the purpose of intervening to change the therapist's behavior are discussed in Chapter 8.

The Supervisor-Observer

As observers, supervisors bring their entire selves to the observation session—including their personal learning histories, their genetic histories, and their present physical and behavioral states. Supervisors' professional histories consist of their personal theory of therapy, their therapy experiences, and their personal theory of supervision. Supervisors should review their own supervision histories from time to time, especially as they prepare to do supervision (see Chapter 2).

As supervisors prepare to do supervision, and especially as they prepare to observe therapists delivering treatment, they augment their personal histories by determining the therapist's preparation for therapy and the supervision goals to be accomplished in this supervision block (see Chapters 3 and 4). With the information about the therapist and the supervision goals as part of their histories, supervisors are ready to begin observing.

Supervision as Experimental Observation

The consultation room may be considered an experimental space for the supervisor. The critical data to be observed in this experimental space is the data generated by the interaction of the therapist and clients. Whether the supervisor observes the session through the one-way screen, on video or audio tape playback, or only hears the scene described by the therapist from the therapist's case notes, the critical variables are the reciprocal exchange of behaviors by the therapist and the clients. Within the consulting room, certain conditions prevail that act as stimuli for both therapists and clients. The conditions that prevail in the consulting room should be the conditions that control the behaviors of all the participants—the behaviors of the therapist, the behaviors of the clients, and the behaviors of the supervisor-observer (Mead & Crane, 1978).

The consulting room as an experimental space. As an experimental space the consulting room presents all the participants with an array of stimuli. The participants respond to the stimulus events and are changed by them.

If the consulting room were a controlled experimental space, some of the stimuli would be determined by the supervisor-experimenter. The stimuli would be standard stimuli presented to determine the response of the participants. We discuss the conditions that might prevail in the consulting room as an experimental space if the therapist's behavior were the standard stimuli presented by an expert therapist, or if the clients' behaviors were the standard stimuli presented by model clients. This is a thought experiment, for as we know, very few of the stimuli presented by either trainee-therapists or by real clients could be considered as standard stimuli. Later, we return to the consulting room as the nonstandard place that it is.

For the supervisor one set of standard conditions for this experimental space would be to have these clients with their specific class of problems in the consulting room with an expert exemplar therapist (Gilbert, 1978). The exemplar therapist's behavior would then act as a standard. The performance of the exemplar therapist serves as a model or template against which the therapist-trainee's performance of delivering therapy will be evaluated. Successful supervision occurs when the supervisor can help the therapist to deliver therapy that matches the performance of the expert exemplar.

Another mark of successful supervision is when the supervisor can help the therapist deliver therapy that produces the same outcomes as would be produced by the expert exemplar. The clients' responses to the standard stimuli presented by the exemplar therapist would fall within a predictable range of behaviors. The more closely the therapist-trainee's behavior matches that of the exemplar, the more closely will the outcome for the clients match that achieved by the exemplar.

Theoretically, the clients could be placed in this experimental observation space with an almost infinite number of expert therapists, each of whom could be an exemplar of a different model of therapy.

Clinically, the choice of an exemplar might be limited to one who is an expert in presenting an empirically tested treatment for the given class of problems and types of clients. If no empirically tested treatment exists, an exemplar of a theoretically derived treatment would be applied.

The choice of theoretical models, and thus of exemplars, may be limited to the model specified by the training agency. But even if the number of models of therapy the therapist may learn are open in this setting, the supervisor may be limited to an exemplar that matches the supervisor's preferred model of therapy. However, if the supervisor has developed an eclectic model, and the system is open, then the expert exemplar to be used may be negotiated when supervisor and therapist are establishing the supervision goals.

The supervisor who observes the events in the consulting room needs to balance both sides of the equation. On one side of the equation we have the behavior of the exemplar therapist acting as a stimulus for the behavior of the clients. On the other side of the equation we have the behavior of the clients acting as a stimulus for the therapist. These are reciprocating sets of contingencies, they are not mirror images of each other. Therefore, for the supervisor another set of standard conditions for the consulting room as an experimental space might be for the clients to be model clients.

Model clients would provide a constant set of stimulus events to the therapist-trainee. The supervisor could then observe the therapist's responses to the standard stimuli and could then easily diagnose the therapist's skills, strengths, and deficits in delivering a specified therapy.

For the consulting room as an experimental space, the model clients would be of a particular type with a specified set of dysfunctional behaviors. For example, the clients' type might be a white middle-class couple, age 33, with a college education. Their dysfunctional pattern might be a classical case of marital conflict. For training purposes it would be nice to have model clients for all possible combinations of types of dysfunctions therapists might encounter, such as younger, middle-aged, older male and female depressed clients, and so on. The supervisor's task in establishing the goals for supervision would be to determine, with the therapist, those combinations of client types and dysfunctional patterns with which the therapist needs to practice prior to seeing "real" clients. The appropriate model clients would then be selected to elicit therapist responses for training.

The supervisor could then observe the model clients providing standard stimulus conditions to the therapist-trainee. The trainee's performance would then be compared to responses made by expert exemplar therapists and the supervisor would reinforce the trainee for behaviors that approximate those of the exemplars. The trainees would be encouraged to continue to respond until their responses duplicated those of the exemplars.

At present, expert exemplar therapists probably exist only in the minds of supervisors and we have only a few simulated model clients (Butcher, Scofield, & Baker, 1984, 1985; Mead, 1985; Newsom, 1986; Valentine, 1986). However, even if we had all possible combinations of types of client problems simulated, they would only serve for training. Supervision would still be required to help therapists shift from the model clients to real, live clients. The task of supervision is to help therapists deliver therapy to real clients.

The consulting room as a nonstandard space. What really happens in the supervisor's experimental space, that is, what the supervisor observes occurring in the consulting room, is this: Therapist-trainees encounter real clients. There are no standard conditions. The trainees are not expert therapists and the clients are not model clients. Therefore, the supervisor must determine, by observation, the nature of the stimulation the clients are providing the therapist. That is, the supervisor must make an assessment or diagnosis of the client type and the class of problems being presented which is independent of the assessment or diagnosis made by the therapist. The supervisor's assessment is akin to the assessment made by the exemplar therapist. The supervisor must also determine, through observation, the nature of the therapist's responses to the stimuli presented by the clients and then assess how near the trainee's response is to the one that would be offered by the supervisor as exemplar therapist. The necessity for these types of observations makes this work one of the principal tasks of supervision.

Clients as nonstandard stimuli. The supervisor observes the therapist-trainee being confronted by real clients who rarely present with textbook cases of anything. The clients provide stimuli for therapists all right, but the stimuli are a confusing, often conflicting, array of sensory stimuli. These stimuli may be simultaneously perceived by the therapist as affective, behavioral, and cognitive messages.

Supervisors are aware that clients bring their complete selves to the consulting room. The clients' selves consist of their genetic histories, their personal histories, and their current set of controlling variables, just as we saw for supervisors. Perhaps the most important part of the clients' personal histories is their family histories. These histories are derived from each spouse's family of origin and from this family, the family of procreation. For many clients the most important controlling variables in their lives are the reciprocal exchange of contingencies with other family members. Some of these exchanges may lead to dysfunctional behavior on the part of one or more family members. This dysfunctional behavior is shaped and maintained by the interaction of the family members with each other.

The clients, as family members, bring their system of exchanging reciprocal contingencies to therapy and this system is a powerful controller of behavior. When family members as clients are presented with the therapist as a stimulus object, they may respond to the therapist much as they would to another family member. In the process of exchanging reciprocal contingencies with the therapist, the clients provide the therapist with stimuli, some of which are reinforcing and some of which are punishing. The therapist may be *reinforced* by the clients for appropriate therapist behavior, but he or she may also be reinforced for inappropriate therapist behavior. In the same way, the therapist may get *punished* for appropriate therapist behavior or may get punished for inappropriate therapist behavior. The unwary therapist may be preempted into the clients' ongoing system, especially if the clients are two or more members of a family. As Skinner (1953) has noted, two or more people acting in concert may exert a powerful controlling influence over the behavior of a third person.

The therapist-trainee as a nonstandard stimulus. Just as the supervisor observes the clients, the supervisor simultaneously observes that the therapist provides stimuli for the clients. The therapist brings his or her self to the consulting room, just as do clients and supervisors. The therapist's personal and professional histories are part of that self. When the therapist encounters the clients in the consulting room, the therapist provides family members with stimuli based upon her or his history and her or his perception of the stimuli presented by the clients. The therapist may provide the clients with *reinforcement* for appropriate and functional behavior or for inappropriate and dysfunctional behavior. The therapist's behavior may also serve as *punishment* to the clients for appropriate and functional behavior or as punishment for inappropriate and dysfunctional behavior.

As the supervisor-observer views clients' behaviors as controlling variables for the therapist's behavior and the therapist's behavior as controlling variables for the clients, the supervisor's task is to determine if the therapist's behavior is proving to be therapeutic to the clients. While observing the therapist, the supervisor is aware of the therapist's professional strengths, weaknesses, level of experience, and the supervision goals. Each of these variables is part of the equation that the supervisor must use to determine if the therapist's performance is effective.

Balancing this equation are the client variables. The supervisor is becoming aware, along with the therapist, of the clients' strengths and weaknesses, personal styles, therapy experience, specific dysfunctional patterns, goals for therapy, expectations for outcomes, and so on. The therapist's performance must be evaluated against difficulties presented by these less than model clients.

Observing Therapists' Treatment Delivery

One of the challenges for the supervisor is to make sense out of all this. One way to understand what is going on is to start with awareness of the Task-Oriented Model. As the supervisor begins his or her observations of the therapist's and clients' exchanges in the consulting room, the supervisor asks herself or himself what tasks, from the client level of the Task-Oriented Model (see Level 1, Figure 2.1), are appropriate for these clients at this time. For example, is the task that the clients must complete with the therapist, "establishing the nature of the problem and the goals for therapy"? Or is the task, "putting the treatment plan into practice"?

Once the supervisor has determined the appropriate client task, the supervisor asks what tasks from Level 2 of the Task-Oriented Model are appropriate for the therapist to be performing at this time? The supervisor can then observe to see if the therapist is performing the correct ones.

The supervisor must also consider the goals of supervision related to the observations of the therapist's treatment delivery. The supervisor must ask him- or herself if the therapist's performance observed in the therapy session is moving the therapist toward the goals established in the supervision plan. In addition, the supervisor must determine the therapist's perceptions of his or her treatment delivery and its impact upon the clients. This can best be done by interviewing the therapist.

INTERVIEWING THERAPISTS
TO DETERMINE THEIR CLINICAL REASONING

Simply observing the tasks being exchanged in an experimental space, such as the consulting room, cannot give the supervisor a complete understanding of the therapist's treatment delivery. To fully understand what is going on, the supervisor must interview the therapist to determine what the therapist is observing about his or her treatment delivery and what the therapist is observing about the impact of the treatment on the clients. This interview will give the supervisor information about the therapist's clinical reasoning.

It is assumed that expert therapists observe their treatment delivery and observe and evaluate the impact of their treatment on the clients. It is also assumed that expert therapists adjust their behavior based upon their observations of the clients' responses to their therapy. Since the therapist's behavior can have a therapeutic, a neutral, or a damaging impact upon the clients (Beutler, Crago, & Arizmendi, 1986), supervisors must help trainees learn to evaluate their own impact and, if the impact is not therapeutic, to change their behavior.

The supervisor must interview the therapist to determine the therapist's clinical reasoning and decision making because much of the information about the therapist's responses to the impact of the treatment on the clients is contained within the therapist. Only the therapist knows what the therapist has observed about the clients. Only the therapist knows what affective responses the therapist is having in response to the behavior of the clients. Only the therapist knows the reasoning the therapist is using to decide how to respond to the changes that are occurring in the clients. The supervisor can only determine what the therapist knows and feels and what the therapist's clinical reasoning is by conducting an interview.

Therapists' Clinical Reasoning About Treatment Delivery

At some point either during or after the therapy session, the supervisor must interview the therapist to determine what the therapist has observed and the therapist's clinical reasoning about those observations. The supervisor may start with a question about the therapist's desired outcomes for this session (see Figure 3.1). Next the supervisor may ask about the data gleaned from his or her observation of the session. The supervisor takes note of the therapist's response to the question about observations and then probes for the therapist's clinical reasoning behind the answers. Having identified the observations the therapist has made, the supervisor may probe to determine the theoretical concepts that the therapist is applying to organize these observations. The supervisor may then compare the therapist's responses in the interview with the therapist's performance observed in the therapy session. The supervisor also compares the therapist's responses with the responses an exemplar therapist might make to the same questions.

The therapist's clinical reasoning about treatment impact. To help the trainee to become an expert therapist, the supervisor must be able to determine how the trainee reasons about his or her impact on the clients. The supervisor also needs to determine the processes the therapist uses in deciding how to act toward the clients as they respond to the therapist's treatment behaviors. Either during the session or after the session, the supervisor may interview the therapist about what the therapist has observed about treatment impact. The supervisor can probe concerning observations the therapist has made about the affective, behavioral, and cognitive responses of the clients to the therapist. The supervisor also inquires about the affective, behavioral, and cognitive responses of the therapist to the clients. The supervisor may further probe to determine the therapist's clinical reasoning concerning the interaction between the client events and the therapist events. The supervisor next questions the therapist about the theoretical concepts she or he is using to explain the impact of the treatment on the behavior of the clients.

The therapist's clinical reasoning about the client and therapist tasks. The supervisor uses questions similar to those in Figure 5.1 (pg. 67) to interview the therapist about the client and therapist tasks that have been completed and those yet to be performed. Once the tasks have been identified, the supervisor may probe to determine the therapist's ability to use clinical reasoning to apply the theoretical model being learned to achieve the tasks. The supervisor can inquire about the variables that the theory puts forth as important in understanding the client's behavior. To connect the therapist's observations to the important theoretical variables, the supervisor should ask which specific client behaviors represent the variables in question. Similarly, the therapist should be asked to identify which of his or her behaviors are expressions of the variables the theory would say should be manipulated to bring about therapeutic change. The supervisor may determine if the therapist has identified all the necessary variables and if the variables are sufficient to explain the client's behavior. The supervisor may inquire about the hypotheses the therapist has formed and the steps she or he has taken or may take to test them. Through careful inquiry, coupled with ample expressions of support and understanding, the supervisor may come to recognize the strengths and limitations of the therapist's clinical reasoning.

Timeliness of the interview. The supervisor will generally find it helpful to arrange to interview the therapist about his or her responses to the clients as close to the time of the therapy session as possible (Breunlin, Karrer et al., 1988). In this way the affect as well as the content of the session are more likely to be available to the therapist. The supervisor may use special techniques such as those developed by Kagan (1980) and others (Kramer & Reitz, 1980; Whiffen, 1982) to help process the therapist's affective responses to the clients. Most of these approaches are designed to help the therapist reexperience the events of the therapy session in the supervision session by systematically using video tape excerpts to prompt the therapist to recall the content and the associated affect.

The observation and interviewing procedures described have been most applicable to live supervision, co-therapy, or tape review supervision. Other techniques need to be considered when the more traditional case review approach to supervision is used.

Determining Therapist Behavior from Case Note Presentations

Case note presentation is perhaps the most often used form of supervision (Wetchler, Piercy, & Sprenkle, 1989). As with the other forms of supervision, the purpose of case note presentations is to increase the competence of the therapist. To be effective the therapist should write out the case notes and then present them to the supervisor. The case notes should be organized, systematic, and subject to verification. To be organized the case notes must follow some consistent format. To be systematic they must be kept routinely for every session of every case. For the purpose of verification, the case notes must be clear, specific descriptions of observable events, and they must indicate the source of the information. Clarity and specification means the avoidance of generalizations and jargon. This approach ensures that information can be returned to for new hypotheses as often as needed, whereas case notes that consist only of inferences or vaguaries yield too little information to build upon for further analysis (Bromley, 1977; Nelson & Barlow, 1981). For example, notes that state, "Ronnie was elated," are too vague and do not indicate their source. Better notes might say, "The therapist observed Ronnie squirming in his chair, grinning, laughing, and speaking cheerfully to all who would listen," or the notes could state, "Ronnie reported that he was 'never so happy in all his life.'" Both of the latter examples are clear, specific descriptions of behavior that indicate the source of the information and as such they allow one to return to the information for additional hypotheses. The statement "Ronnie was elated" is a dead end.

Several authors have provided helpful discussions of case note taking (Nelson & Barlow, 1981; Presser & Pfost, 1985; Sprenkle & Fisher, 1978) and report writing (Bromley, 1977). These scholars have suggested that case note taking can help therapists organize their material so that they learn to (a) determine which information is important to observe and report; (b) form hypotheses about the behavior of the clients, the clients' interaction, the therapist's behavior, and the interaction of the therapist with the clients; (c) conceptualize the case by putting the observations into a theoretical perspective; (d) establish treatment plans; and (e) evaluate progress and outcome (Presser & Pfost, 1985; Sprenkle & Fisher, 1978).

Not only do case notes benefit the clients and the therapist as already described, they also serve to help the therapist to communicate about the case with other therapists. Case notes are useful when the therapist needs to communicate with others in case consultation, supervision, or when referring the case. Finally, case notes also serve as a defense for the therapist should legal or ethical issues ever arise (Slovenko, 1980).

Case note format. Case notes can be organized into eight basic sections designed to help therapists achieve the results previously discussed. A sample format for written case notes appears in Figure 6.1. A similar form can be constructed in a word processor as a merge letter and case notes can be typed directly into the form for easy storage and printing. The case note sections include: (1) session summary; (2) client observations; (3) therapist observations; (4) therapist-client interaction; (5) problems addressed; (6) interventions and progress made; (7) homework assigned; and (8) plans, goals, and strategies (Presser & Pfost, 1985; Sprenkle & Fisher, 1978). A brief discussion of the sections follows.

1. Session Summary. This section is a brief narrative report of the session in which the therapist presents the highlights of the session sequentially. Brevity is key here; therefore, therapists are encouraged to be careful to discriminate among the session events and to select only clinically relevant material.

2. Client Observations. This section is composed of two subsections; the first is for the recording of the observations of the clients' verbal and nonverbal behaviors, and the second is used to record the therapist's conceptualizations about the data recorded in the observations subsection. As stated previously, the recording of the observations

(continued on p. 93)

Client No._____ Clients Present_____

Date_____ Session No._____

Therapist_____ Supervisor_____

I. Session Summary

II. Clients

A. Observations

B. Conceptualization:
Inferences & Hypotheses

Figure 6.1 Confidential Case Progress Notes

III. Therapist

A. Observations   B. Conceptualization:
                                      Inferences & Hypotheses

IV. Therapist-Client Interactions

A. Observations   B. Conceptualization:
                                      Inferences & Hypotheses

V. Problems Addressed

(continued)

VI. Interventions and Progress

A. Interventions   B. Progress

VII. Homework

A. Assigned   B. Progress

VIII. Plans, Goals, and Strategies

(N. R. Presser and K. S. Pfost [1985]. A format for individual psychotherapy notes. *Professional Psychology: Research and Practice, 16*(1), 11–16. Copyright 1985 by the American Psychological Association. Adapted by permission.)

about the clients should be objective and specific, and should indicate the source. The therapist should discriminate between the clinically relevant information and the other information shared by the clients in the session. The therapist should focus on the affective, behavioral, and cognitive issues that the client reports. In the case of family therapy the therapist should report the amount of agreement and disagreement about these issues family members express (Sprenkle & Fisher, 1978). Behavioral patterns of interaction among family members should be recorded here. Test scores and objective measures such as weight or numbers of hours of sleep at night should also be recorded here.

Once the objective data base has been established, the therapist may list inferences and hypotheses about the client data in the conceptualization subsection of the clients' section of the case notes form. In the therapist's conceptualization subsection, the therapist may wish to speculate upon the meaning and value of the issues for each family member. He or she may also record his or her interpretations of the family members' rules, patterns of control used and attempted, support used and attempted, communication strengths and weaknesses, problem-solving methods used, and so on.

3. Therapist Observations. This section is also composed of two subsections, the therapist's self-observations and the therapist's conceptualizations about those observations. The first subsection is used to record the therapist's perceptions and observations of self using his or her five senses. Both verbal and nonverbal affective, behavioral, and cognitive responses on the part of the therapist should be observed and recorded. The therapist differentiates between his or her responses in the session and those of the clients.

In the second therapist subsection, the therapist may speculate about the internal consistency of his or her behavior, the relationship of the behavior to his or her personal theoretical model, and the evolution of his or her own integrated personal style of therapy (Presser & Pfost, 1985).

4. Therapist-Client Interaction. This section is also divided into two subsections, observations of the therapist-client interactions, and the therapist's conceptualizations of those observations. The assumptions here is that the reciprocal exchange of contingencies, between clients and therapist and therapist and clients, is important to record to determine the therapist's observation of, and conceptualization of, the impact of the treatment on the clients (Chapter 7). This section can be useful in understanding the system dynamics of the family as the family processes are experienced by the therapist. In the observations subsection the behavioral sequences between therapist and clients and clients and therapist need to be observed and the related affective and cognitive issues specified.

In the therapist-client interaction conceptualization subsection, the therapist may make inferences and hypotheses about his or her responses to the family members for diagnostic purposes (Presser & Pfost, 1985). In the conceptualization subsection, the therapist should record his or her interpretations of the rules, patterns of control used and attempted, support used and attempted, communication strengths and weaknesses, and problem-solving methods used in the sequences that include the therapist as part of the therapist-clients system. Therapists should be aware of the findings from attributions theory that suggest that individuals tend to attribute external causes (state or situational variables) to their behavior, and internal causes (trait or dispositional variables) to other people's behavior when looking at interaction sequences (Presser & Pfost, 1985). Clear and specific reporting of behavioral sequences rather than inferences and hypotheses should lessen this form of bias.

5. Problems Addressed. This section lists problems that were specifically addressed *in this therapy session*. The problems should be clearly stated and each family member's point of view described (Sprenkle & Fisher, 1978). Sources of the information should be identified. This section is directly related to the subsequent sections.

6. Interventions and Progress. This section is comprised of the interventions subsection and the progress subsection. The interventions should follow rationally and logically from the observations and the conceptualizations derived from those observations that were reported in the earlier sections of the case notes. The interventions should be addressed to specific problems. In the progress subsection the therapist should provide evidence for progress from multiple sources and using multiple means. Subjective self-reports, paper and pencil instruments, counts of target behaviors, physiological measures, and ratings by outside observers should all be included whenever applicable.

7. Homework Assigned. The work of therapy, to be successful, must extend in time and space beyond the consulting room. Homework is one way to move the therapy out of the exclusive domain of consulting room and into the home. Homework also extends the time of therapy beyond the 50-minute-hour. Homework should be based upon the same considerations as other interventions. It should be clear and specific. It should flow logically from the observational data base and from the therapist's conceptualizations of that data.

The homework should be evaluated for progress in the same way that other interventions are evaluated, that is, by multiple sources and by multiple methods.

8. *Plans, Goals, and Strategies.* This section is a place for therapists to make notes "to themselves." Items that do not seem to fit logically anywhere else can be entered in this section (Presser & Pfost, 1985). For example, telephone notes may be entered here and correspondence may be attached.

To be useful for supervision, case notes must be seen as a summary and an analysis of each therapy interview rather than simply as a quick reference for the therapist (Sprenkle & Fisher, 1978). As summary and analysis, the case notes set the stage for the case note presentation supervision session. If the case notes are delivered to the supervisor prior to the session, the supervisor can be prepared to hold a meaningful interview with the trainee. This interview may follow the procedures described for understanding the therapist's clinical reasoning or the interview may be held to prepare the supervisor to intervene with the therapist.

In conclusion, the principal tasks of supervision appear to be the supervisor's observations and analyses of the events that occur within the experimental space of the consulting room. Within that space therapist and clients reciprocally exchange behaviors and change each other. To fully understand the events that occur in the consulting room, the supervisor must observe both the therapist and the clients, and then interview the therapist. The supervisor uses the interview to determine the therapist's clinical reasoning associated with his or her performance in the therapy session. Only by combining the information received by observing the events in the consulting room with the information gained from the interviews with the therapist can the supervisor begin to understand the behavior that is occurring in this experimental space.

Once the supervisor has come to understand the nature of the events in the consulting room, she or he will be ready to formulate some interventions to change the behavior of the therapist to resemble that of the exemplar therapist. It is assumed that when the therapist-trainee's delivery of treatment comes to resemble that of an expert exemplar therapist, then the outcomes for the clients will be similar to those expected with the expert therapist. The goal of the supervisor is to bring the therapist-trainee's performance in line with the performance of an expert therapist. How the supervisor intervenes to attempt to bring about changes in the therapist's behavior is discussed in Chapter 7.

Evaluating and Intervening in Therapist Behaviors

INTRODUCTION

In Chapter 6 we consider the supervisor's tasks of observing the therapist delivering treatment, determining the impact of treatment on the clients, and interviewing the therapist to determine the therapist's clinical reasoning. In this chapter we extend the supervisor's use of observation and interviewing from gathering information to (a) evaluating the therapist's progress and (b) forming interventions to improve the therapist's performance.

EVALUATING THE THERAPIST'S PROGRESS

The process of therapist evaluation suggests comparisons of the therapist's performance with some criteria. The criteria for evaluation of the therapist should have been determined in the supervision plan. As Kaslow (1977) states therapist evaluation requires supervision goals that are measurable, observable, and that may be operationalized. In addition, therapist evaluation should be taken from all three levels of the Task-Oriented Model (see Figure 2.1). Multilevel and multimethod evaluation seems most likely to give the supervisor the complete view of the therapist's performance (Kaslow, 1977; Styczynski, 1980). Therefore, assessment of therapist progress, which is the focus of this chapter, and assessment of therapist outcome,

96

which is the focus of Chapter 8, should include evaluations by the clients, by the therapist, and by the supervisor.

As suggested in earlier chapters the top level goals of supervision are to help therapists become expert therapists and to protect the welfare of the clients. More specific supervision goals are determined by the profession, the state, and by the administrative units of the agency in which the supervision is performed. Finally, even more specific goals are developed by the therapist and the supervisor as they work together to establish the supervision plan. The supervisor observes the therapist attempting to achieve these goals as the therapist interacts with the clients in the therapy session. The supervisor then evaluates the therapist's performance against the performance of an exemplar therapist. The supervisor then intervenes to improve the therapist's performance or if needed to protect the client's welfare.

Observing and Intervening

The client level of the Task-Oriented Model. In order to carry out the tasks of supervision the supervisor needs much of the same kind of information about the clients that the therapist needs. However, whereas the therapist needs this information to perform therapy, the supervisor needs it to supervise the therapist-trainee. The supervisor needs to observe the behavior about which the clients are complaining—the behavior that causes the clients to come to therapy (Baer, 1986). The supervisor needs to have this information in order to evaluate the therapist's skill in observing the nature of the clients' presenting problems. The supervisor also requires information about the clients' behavior to compare the supervisor's assessment of the clients' problems with the assessment made by the therapist (Spitzer et al., 1982).

In making observations of the clients, the supervisor must keep in mind that it is the therapist's responsibility to do the therapy and it is the supervisor's job to supervise. Although the same types of information are needed by the supervisor and the therapist, the supervisor generally does not act directly on that information. When the impact of the therapist's treatment on the clients is not therapeutic the supervisor should intervene, not with the clients, but with the therapist. The supervisor's interventions must take into account the clients' welfare, but they must also consider the supervision goals designed to help the therapist learn new skills in delivering therapy. The supervisor must ask himself or herself, not, "How can I help these clients?", but, "How can I change this therapist so that the therapist can help these clients?"

For example, it is the therapist's responsibility to determine which assessments and procedures to use to formulate and test hypotheses about the nature of the clients' problems. It is the supervisor's responsibility to determine that the therapist has used good clinical judgment in the selection of the assessments and procedures to be used. To evaluate the therapist's clinical judgment, the supervisor must observe the clients to determine if the therapist's selection of assessments and procedures is appropriate.

The therapist level of the Task-Oriented Model. The supervisor may request an interview with the therapist prior to the first session with the clients. In preparation for this interview, the supervisor may ask the therapist to be ready to discuss the procedures and assessment instruments he or she plans to use in the first sessions. In order to understand the therapist's clinical reasoning, the supervisor will need to probe with questions designed to get the therapist to share what he or she plans to do and why. As the therapist reviews his or her selection of procedures and assessment instruments, the supervisor compares the therapist's choices with those an expert therapist might make with similar clients with similar problems.

When the supervisor asks the therapist why he or she plans to do something, the supervisor is asking for a conceptualization (Cleghorn & Levin, 1973; Tomm & Wright, 1979). One purpose of clarifying the therapist's conceptualization of the case is to evaluate his or her use of a clinical or theoretical model to organize observations rather than simply reacting to the clients out of personal biases.

The process of conceptualizing a case into a theoretical model is difficult, especially for therapists at beginning and middle experience levels. The therapist may be unable to place the information from this case into a specific therapy model. In situations where the therapist is unable to conceptualize the case, the supervisor may help by using questions similar to those found in Figure 5.1. The supervisor may guide the therapist's thinking by means of prompts and probes about the relevant variables according to the theory in question, how those variables are operationalized, how those variables are manifest in this specific case, what those variables suggest about the most probable treatment in this case, and what the variables indicate about probable outcomes.

More experienced therapists may propose a theoretical explanation that is outside of the model being used in the given training center or training block. If the discussion about theoretical models is not handled well, therapist and supervisor could get into a clash of paradigms. When the therapist proposes one model of therapy and the supervisor another, they may each end up being defensive and resistant to learning from one another.

The probability of a paradigm clash between supervisor and therapist may be reduced by asking the therapist to identify, from the Task-Oriented Model, what the therapist believes to be the necessary task for the clients at this time (see Figure 2.1). By focusing first on the general procedural task, rather than on the therapist's theory, the therapist is less likely to be personally committed and, therefore, less likely to be defensive and resistant. When the therapist has identified the task correctly, the supervisor may then ask what procedures the therapist plans to use to accomplish that task. Next the supervisor may probe to determine how those procedures were deduced from the theory the therapist is using. If the therapist responds with a model other than the one currently being taught, the supervisor may ask the therapist to compare the procedures that may be deduced from the model being taught to the model described by the trainee. The supervisor and therapist may then work together to determine the best approach for these clients with their specific problems and the best approach for the therapist to take to achieve the goals of supervision. After client welfare, the further development of therapist skills is the primary concern of both supervisor and therapist.

Probes that elicit the therapist's clinical reasoning and conceptualization of the case may provide the supervisor with some understanding of how the therapist is connecting the information that is known about the clients to the theory being used and the action proposed. Similarly, the therapist's responses to the supervisor's probes may provide the supervisor with information that may be used (a) to evaluate the therapist's conceptualization of the case, (b) to teach the therapist how to use the model being taught, and (c) to evaluate the therapist's performance in the clinical sessions conducted by the therapist following the supervision session.

When the supervisor has helped the therapist to clarify and specify the tasks to be accomplished in the next therapy sessions, the therapist is prepared to go into the consulting room and deliver the treatment. Under these circumstances both supervisor and therapist are in a position to evaluate the therapist's performance in delivering treatment and to determine if the therapist's treatment resembles the treatment of an exemplar therapist.

The same processes may be used for any therapy task. If, for example, the therapist believes he or she has completed the job of assessing the case and determining the clients' problems and goals, the supervisor may check out the therapist's clinical reasoning about these tasks using questions such as those described in Figure 3.1 and Figure 5.1. Does the therapist have enough data? All of the data? Too much data? If data is missing, how will the therapist go about collecting it most efficiently? What assumptions about the case information is the therapist making? What hypotheses has the therapist formed? Which hypotheses has the therapist tested? How were they tested? What does the therapist see as the treatment of choice? What is the basis of the therapist's selection of the treatment plan? Is the treatment plan consistent with the theory being applied? Is the plan consistent with the current available information about the clients and their specific problems? What does the therapist see as the next task? How does the therapist propose to achieve that task? Again, it is the therapist's job to collect and evaluate the data, formulate hypotheses, and formulate the treatment plan. It is the supervisor's job to evaluate how successfully or unsuccessfully the therapist has completed these tasks. Success may be measured against the hypothesized performance of an expert exemplar therapist using the most appropriate clinical or theoretical model.

Matching Information to the Goals of Supervision

The task of the supervisor is to help the therapist's treatment delivery match that of the exemplar therapist. To accomplish this task the supervisor needs specific types of information. The type of information one wishes to collect determines how one will collect it. For example, suppose one of the supervision goals is for the therapist to learn how to treat families in which at least one member of the family is depressed. The supervisor should have collected information about the therapist's understanding of the general functions of depression in families during the development of the therapist data base. If information about the therapist's understanding about the effects and treatment of depression in the family was not collected at that time, then this is one of the places where the supervisor loops back to complete an earlier supervision task (Level 3, Figure 2.1). Therapist data base information is generally collected outside of the therapy sessions by interviewing the therapist or by administering paper and pencil assessments to the therapist. Therefore, if the depression in this family is anticipated by the intake notes or in some other way, the supervision task of determining the therapist's preparation to treat depression should be completed by the supervisor prior to the therapist seeing the clients. If the depression was not anticipated and is determined in the therapist's clinical session, then the supervisor may need to determine the therapist's capacity to handle the problem between sessions, if the condition of the clients makes this possible. However, if the clients are at immediate risk, the supervisor may need to take over the case until the therapist is ready, or the supervisor may help the therapist to refer the case to another therapist who is prepared to handle the problem.

Should the supervisor determine that the therapist is prepared to handle the depression in the family, she or he may need information to evaluate what the therapist understands about the impact of depression on a family member in this specific family. Information about the function of depression in the family can be gathered in several ways, depending upon how the supervisor plans to use that information to evaluate and intervene with the therapist. The supervisor can ask the therapist to describe the functions served by the depression in this family. The supervisor can ask to see any assessment data related to the depression of specific family members. And the supervisor can observe the family.

If the supervisor wants information to determine if the therapist can give a verbal description of the depressed family member, the therapist's self-report may suffice. The supervisor asks the therapist for a verbal description of the functions served by the depression in this family and the therapist responds with a verbal description. The supervisor may ask probing questions about the therapist's personal responses to the family members, the nature of the affect expressed by the members of the family, the therapist's affective responses to the family members, and so on. Based upon this information, the supervisor may attempt to verify the assessment, make recommendations to the therapist about how to improve his or her therapeutic responses to the family, or determine the progress the therapist has made toward becoming expert in the treatment of families with a depressed member. However, if the supervisor is attempting to accomplish these latter tasks, then some form of information other than verbal self-reports may be required.

The method the supervisor has used to collect supervision information may help or hinder the supervisor when he or she attempts to (a) evaluate the reliability and validity of the information the therapist is using to make decisions; (b) evaluate the correctness of the therapist's assessment; (c) determine the appropriateness of the therapist's responses; and (d) determine the progress the therapist is making in his or her skill in treating families with any specific treatment program. Recall that Spitzer et al. (1982) found that supervisors who attempted to make an assessment of the case based upon the information supervisees presented were often in error. The information the supervisor receives from the therapist's self-reports is limited to the extent and accuracy of the observations made by the therapist and the therapist's skill in reporting observations.

What is true of the therapist's self-reports about assessment would also appear to be true of the therapist's self-reports about her or his treatment delivery. Therefore, the supervisor needs to establish procedures to determine the reliability and validity of the therapist's account of delivery of the treatment to the clients. Changes in the clients' pre- and post-therapy assessment instrument scores may help answer the question, "Was the therapist's treatment helpful?" However, if the supervisor relies upon the pre- and post-treatment assessment instruments, the question must be put in the past tense. If the supervisor wants to know the impact of the treatment the therapist is delivering right now, then it is necessary to have some continuous measures of client progress and to observe the therapist's treatment delivery.

In conclusion, it appears that to achieve the supervision goals it will be necessary for the supervisor to obtain data not only from the therapist's self-reports, but from assessment instruments administered to both the therapist and the clients, and from observations of the therapist's and client's interaction in the session. The multi-method approach seems to be the only logical way to go about answering the questions the supervisor needs to ask to assess events at all levels of the supervisor-therapist-client system.

INTERVENING IN SUPERVISION

Following the observations and interviews with the therapist, the supervisor may make one of three classes of responses. First, the supervisor may do nothing. Second, the supervisor may reinforce a correct response or punish an incorrect one. And third, the supervisor may work to expand the therapist's range of behaviors. Each of these responses may be considered as a class of interventions.

Doing Nothing

The supervisor's doing nothing is not a null or empty response in terms of the supervisor-therapist system. The therapist may interpret the supervisor's doing nothing as disapproval or lack of concern, both of which may be taken as punishment (Loeber & Weisman, 1975). Therefore, since the supervisor has a high probability of doing nothing following a correct response, the supervisor may wish to define "not responding" as approval (Loeber & Weisman, 1975).

When the therapist first responds correctly in the sessions using a new technique or performing a new skill, the supervisor may respond with words of encouragement and praise. Encouragement and praise are often reinforcing. However, after a period of time there is a diminished probability that the supervisor will continue to reinforce and praise the therapist's performance of a technique or skill that occurs at some relatively high frequency (Loeber & Weisman, 1975). The supervisor's attention is turned to other skills and techniques. This shift to doing nothing following a well-learned response on the part of the therapist should be interpreted as approval and satisfaction with the therapist's performance.

Reinforcing and Punishing

The supervisor may reinforce correct therapist behaviors and punish incorrect ones by providing "corrective" feedback. Feedback may be immediate in live supervision or delayed in the other forms of supervision. Reinforcement, as mentioned above, may first come in the form of verbal behavior which may be classed as approval, praise, and encouragement. Behavior of the so-called "nonverbal" type is also included here. For example, a smile, a thumbs up sign, an "O.K." sign, or a nod may all serve as positive reinforcement for a job well done.

An important part of reinforcement comes from the type of corrective feedback known as "pointing up contingencies of reinforcement" (Skinner, 1953). The supervisor makes statements such as, "Did you notice that when you reflected the client's feelings she began to explore that side of her life more and more?" The supervisor begins to make positive client change reinforcing for the therapist by helping the therapist connect his or her therapeutic behavior in the sessions with changes in the client's behavior.

Since the supervisor's goal is to help the therapist become an expert therapist, the supervisor must work to make the therapist self-correcting and self-reinforcing (Bernstein, Hofmann, & Wade, 1986; Bernstein & Lecomte, 1979a; Keller & Protinsky, 1984). Therefore, the supervisor must attempt to develop the therapist's skills in self-observation as well as in observing clients. By pointing up the contingencies between the therapist's behavior and the clients' behavior the supervisor can help the therapist become self-correcting. Therapist behavior that is associated with no change, or change in the wrong direction, should be followed by changes in the therapist's behaviors.

The therapist first learns to recognize the need for changes in her or his behavior by receiving corrective feedback from the supervisor. The supervisor may start by asking the therapist to discuss what went well and what did not go so well in the session. In this way the supervisor can determine how perceptive the therapist is about the events of the session. After pointing up and reinforcing what the therapist is doing well, the supervisor may turn to the part of the session that did not go so well. Using prompts and probes such as those found in Figure 5.1, the supervisor helps the therapist recognize the variables and their relationship to the treatment to be applied. Alternative therapist behaviors that may prove more appropriate for clients of the type in question with the types of problems being treated can then be explored. As the therapist becomes more and more capable of perceiving the impact of his or her behavior on the clients, the supervisor can begin teaching the therapist to be self-correcting when needed.

The therapist needs to learn self-soothing as well as self-correcting behaviors that may be applied in session (Bernstein, Hofmann, & Wade, 1986; Bernstein & Lecomte, 1979a; Keller, & Protinsky, 1984). When the therapist determines that the treatment delivery is being counter-therapeutic or is meeting with resistance from the clients, then the therapist must start with some self-soothing techniques to avoid building up an excessive load of anxiety. The supervisor may recommend that the therapist start with taking two or three slow, deep breaths and then letting them out gradually. While doing this the therapist should review the steps she or he has taken that appear to be correct and that appear to be helpful. The trainee should be encouraged to deliver self-reinforcement for the correct treatment procedures he or she has delivered. This may be done by giving herself or himself praise and approval for the parts of the job that have been done correctly and well. Next the therapist should review the information being received that is related to the treatment failure and the client resistance. Resistance often comes in the form of failure of the clients to actively take part in the session or some other form of withdrawal, negative comments about the therapist, the therapist's skills, or the treatment, and failure to complete homework (Patterson, 1985).

Once the therapist has determined the source of the problem, the supervisor should encourage the therapist to consider at least three alternative procedures that could be used to accomplish the therapy task required at this time with these clients. The therapist is then encouraged to select the best solution and put it into practice. The therapist should receive the support of the supervisor in carrying out this process and should also be encouraged to learn to use his or her peers in the supervision class or elsewhere for support in continuing to deliver appropriate treatment in spite of client resistance (Patterson, 1985).

Expanding the Therapist's Range

Expanding the therapist's range of therapeutic responses may require the supervisor to intervene with more than doing nothing and reinforcing or punishing responses the therapist is already disposed to emit. The supervisor may need to lecture, assign readings, model, role play, assign simulations, or in some other way intervene to get the therapist to perform some technique that is new to the therapist. Each of the classes of supervision interventions—doing nothing, punishing or reinforcing, and working to expand the therapist's range—takes place within the consulting room or in relationship to the events that occur in the consulting room. In Chapter 6 we considered the consulting room as the supervisor's experimental space. It appears useful to continue that metaphor here as we consider ways the supervisor may intervene to expand the therapist's range of therapeutic responses.

Dependent variables in supervision. Within the supervisor's experimental space there are two sets of dependent or outcome variables to consider. The first set of outcome variables is comprised of the clients' behaviors. The therapist's treatment delivery behaviors make up the second set of outcome variables. From the supervisor's point of view, the therapist's treatment delivery behaviors are intermediate variables. This is because the therapist's behavior, when delivered as treatment, is expected to change the behavior of the clients. Therefore, the independent variable in the supervisor-therapist-client system is the supervisor's behavior. The supervisor's interventions are attempts to manipulate the independent variables that control the therapist's behavior in the supervisor's experimental space, the consulting room.

Independent variables in supervision. What are the independent variables that are available to the supervisor and to the therapist to control the therapist's behavior in the consulting room? As discussed in Chapter 1, Mead and Crane (1978) identified five classes of variables that control the therapist's behavior in the consulting room: (1) setting variables, (2) client variables, (3) therapist history, (4) supervisor's behavior, and (5) administrative rules. Not all of these classes of variables are available to the supervisor for manipulation. For example, as pointed out in Chapter 6, the client's behavior is not under the supervisor's control. Also many of the administrative variables established by the agency in which the supervision is taking place are either out of the supervisor's control or only subject to limited manipulation. If there is a range of technical equipment available, such as one-way screens, video, and/or audio recording equipment, then these setting variables are available to the supervisor to manipulate. The use of certain types of supervision observation procedures makes other interventions available to the supervisor, for example, the opportunity to evaluate immediately is possible if the supervision is conducted live from behind a one-way screen. The therapist's history may be subject to the supervisor's manipulations. However, the therapist's history will be slow to change and it changes only as a result of changes in the therapist's behavior in the here-and-now. Therefore, the most accessible variable for the supervisor to manipulate is the supervisor's behavior.

The behavior of the supervisor that can be manipulated to change the behavior of the therapist is largely limited to decisions about how to conduct supervision. If the technical equipment is available, the supervisor may elect to conduct supervision live, with video or audio tape playback, or by case note consultation. The supervisor may elect to be clear and specific in her or his goals and expectations or may elect to leave the goals and expectations unspecified. The supervisor may establish goals unilaterally or may negotiate the goals with the trainee. The supervisor may elect to provide ample and rapid feedback or may elect to provide little or no feedback. The supervisor may choose to provide feedback about errors and weaknesses or may opt to reinforce strengths and successes. The supervisor may decide to lecture, model, and role play, or simply to observe (Stone & Vance, 1976). The supervisor may expect to give advice and directives or the supervisor may elect to probe the trainee to elicit alternate hypotheses, theoretical approaches, techniques, and solutions. The supervisor may choose to recommend readings, viewing tapes of others, interacting with simulations (Mead, 1985; Newsom, 1986; Valentine, 1986; Raasoch & Laqueur, 1979), or the use of other media (Thelen et al., 1979).

It would be nice to think that most successful supervisors blend a little of all of these supervisory interventions to fit the individual learning style of the trainee. However, what actually happens in supervision is not always clear. For example, Yogev and Pion (1984) found that supervisors did not modify their behavior in supervision with beginning trainees and advanced level trainees, whereas others find that supervisors do modify their responses according to therapist levels of experience (Friedlander & Ward, 1984; Worthington, 1984a). There is some evidence that the supervisor's theory of therapy will influence the skills they emphasize (Friedlander & Ward, 1984; Goodyear & Robyak, 1982), although more experienced supervisors are reported to share similar emphases, that is, their responses are not distinguishable on the basis of their theoretical preferences (Goodyear & Robyak, 1982). Less experienced supervisors are more inclined to see trainee behavior as being due to trainee traits rather than due to external events (Worthington, 1984c). Experienced supervisors have been found to generate more planning statements about trainees than inexperienced supervisors, and more of the experienced supervisors' planning statements were about the trainees (Stone, 1980). Beginning supervisors have also been found to differ from each other in their responses to trainees and to vary their own responses from interview to interview (Holloway & Wolleat, 1981). Thus, experienced supervisors appear to vary their behavior according to (a) the level of trainees' skills, (b) the supervisor's model of therapy and supervision, and (c) the supervisor's skill level. This suggests that beginning supervisors may be able to learn to manipulate the variables experienced supervisors manipulate to bring about changes in therapists' behavior. However, considerable research remains to be done to determine exactly what it is that successful supervisors do.

Until the research into what successful experienced supervisors do is completed it will be necessary for supervisors to use interventions that are based upon a theory of supervision. The Task–Oriented Model provides some guidelines to variables that supervisors may use to intervene with therapists. As suggested earlier some of the variables that are available to supervisors are interventions that can be made in ongoing sessions and others are interventions that can be made either pre- or post-session.

Interventions in ongoing sessions. The supervision variables or interventions that are available to the supervisor during ongoing sessions pertain largely to the live supervision method. They include direct intervention with the therapist by means of a "bug-in-the-ear" radio receiver, telephones, knocks on the door, planned exits by the therapist, and supervisor walk-ins. These interventions generally consist of direct or indirect commands from the supervisor to the therapist for certain changes in the therapist's behavior (Mazza, 1988; Wright, 1986).

The commands given by supervisors as interventions may be simple directives, such as, "Ask the mother to comment on the daughter's posture," or they may be for more complex behavior on the part of the therapist, for example, "Consider the task this family needs to achieve next in therapy and take some action that will get them started on it."

While conducting live supervision, if the supervisor observes that the necessary skills required to carry out therapy are not available to the therapist in the session, then the supervisor must make some clinical decisions. Ethically the therapist should not attempt, nor should the supervisor allow the therapist to attempt, to perform treatments for which he or she lacks competence. Therefore, when the supervisor observes the therapist encountering client behaviors in a session for which the therapist is unprepared, the supervisor must act to protect the welfare of the clients.

What alternatives for intervention are open to the supervisor to protect the welfare of the clients? If the session is live the supervisor can intervene directly, as described above. The supervisor can take over the session to various degrees. If the therapist can alter her or his behavior enough by the supervisor giving a few simple directives, then the supervisor may supply some prompts by (a) use of a transmitter to speak into the radio receiver in the therapist's ear, (b) phoning in, or (c) by knocking on the door, depending upon the technology available. If more extensive consultation appears to be needed, the therapist may be invited to step into the observation booth or into a nearby office. Here the supervisor can probe to determine what steps in the process the therapist can do and which steps are likely to block the therapist's performance. If time permits, the supervisor can do the necessary remedial work and send the therapist back in. If it appears that the clients are presenting a problem that will require extensive preparation before the therapist-trainee will be competent to handle it, then the supervisor must make some clinical decisions. These decisions may be made in consultation with the therapist if time permits or the supervisor may decide to make the decisions unilaterally.

The first decision may be to determine whether the problem is such that the clients can be sent home for a few days while the therapist acquires the necessary skills to proceed or whether the problem requires immediate action. If the clients can wait, the supervisor consults with the therapist on terminating the session and then directs the therapist to take the steps necessary to gain the skills needed to continue the treatment. However, if the clients need immediate attention, then the supervisor may take over the session completely by walking in and doing co-therapy.

If the problems presented by the clients will require supervisor and therapist to take a considerable amount of time to make the therapist competent, the supervisor and therapist may decide to refer the case. For example, if a beginning therapist were assigned a couple that complained of marital problems at intake but then revealed in an early session that one of them has an eating disorder, the supervisor might intervene to recommend that the therapist refer the case. The therapist's task would then switch from establishing the client data base to termination and referral procedures. The clients will be served and the beginning therapist will have gained skill in assessment and in making terminations and referrals.

Out-of-session interventions. Out-of-session interventions may apply to live supervision as well as to supervision using video or audio tapes and case note presentations. The procedures described above for intervening by various forms of changes in the supervisor's behavior apply for all of the out-of-session interventions with the exceptions of those supervisor responses that require entering a live session. Out-of-session interventions generally give the supervisor and therapist the luxury of more time to discuss and negotiate alternative responses that the therapist may make in future sessions with the clients. It also gives them time to have a lecturette or model, or to role play or go to the library to review journal articles for the latest techniques to treat specific problems. Even with these options, there are constraints. The clients must receive timely help. Therefore, the therapist must be prepared for the next necessary appointment. How soon the next necessary appointment might be depends upon the nature of the presenting problems. If the presenting problem is depression, the next necessary appointment may be the following day, whereas some other types of problems may be able to wait a week or even two.

The most common forms of out-of-session supervision are discussions of case notes and reviews of video or audio tapes (Wetchler, Piercy, & Sprenkle, 1989). As with other forms of supervision, the purpose of these discussions and reviews is to help the therapist improve his or her skills in delivering therapy and to protect the welfare of the clients.

Although evaluating case notes is an extremely valuable part of supervision, case notes should not be relied upon as the sole source of information to determine if the therapist has made changes in her or his skill in delivering therapy. The problem with relying upon case notes alone is that the supervisor has no way of determining whether the therapist has actually changed his or her treatment delivery behavior or has simply changed how he or she reports events.

Nonetheless, case note writing is an important therapist skill and serves several important purposes. Therefore, supervisors should regularly review the therapist's case notes. One reason for the supervisor to read and evaluate the case notes is to determine if the supervisor needs to intervene to help the therapist improve her or his skill in case note writing. As in other forms of supervision the supervisor may respond with no response, may reinforce or punish the therapist's case note writing, or may seek to improve the therapist's case note writing skills by applying corrective feedback. To determine the therapist's competence in writing case notes requires that the supervisor have some objective criteria against which to evaluate the report. As with other forms of supervision the most readily available source of objective information will be the supervisor's observations of the clients. Therefore, the quality of the case notes depends upon the supervisor's active participation at all levels of the Task-Oriented Model.

The supervisor may also use the case notes to help the therapist improve his or her skills in delivering treatment. For example, the supervisor may use the case notes to determine if the observation sections of the case notes provide enough data to establish the problems and goals for treatment. The problems to be resolved and the goals to be achieved should be clearly and specifically stated.

Any hypotheses about the problems that have been tested should be noted in the case notes along with the method of testing and the results. To illustrate, the supervisor should review the data base for evidence that the therapist has considered whether there is information to support or refute hypotheses of dangerousness, suicidal ideation, organic disabilities, psychosis, and chemical dependency. Hypotheses related to other physical causes of specific behaviors in the presenting problem should be considered, such as diabetes in the case of sexual dysfunctions, and vision and hearing deficits for children with school difficulties. Many of these hypotheses can be tested by asking appropriate questions in the intake assessment instrument or in the intake and initial interviews. The point here is that the supervisor should determine in the case notes that the therapist has considered these hypotheses and has tested them in some way. If the information is not in the case notes, the supervisor should interview the therapist to determine if the therapist observed the relevant information or overlooked it. Here again, the supervisor must have an objective source of information to determine what information is missing. The most readily available source of such information will probably be the supervisor's observations.

The conceptualization sections of the case notes should give the supervisor insight into the therapist's use of clinical methods and theory. The concepts used to organize the data and to establish additional hypotheses should be tied to the information in the observation sections. The supervisor should challenge the therapist's skills in conceptualizing the case by asking questions, such as those outlined in Figures 3.1 and 5.1, related to the objective data and the therapist's statements in the conceptualization sections of the case notes.

A treatment plan designed to resolve the problems and achieve the goals should be present in the case notes after the initial interviews have been completed. As with the case notes, the treatment plan should indicate the information that forms the basis of the hypotheses about problems and goals. The treatments designed to alleviate the problems and reach the goals should be directly connected to those problems and goals and should be based upon a clinical or theoretical model.

Finally, the case notes should contain regular progress notes that indicate when specific steps of the treatment plan were initiated and how and when progress has been assessed. Case notes constructed and used in this way should benefit the clients and should prove useful in helping therapists to better learn how to deliver and evaluate therapy.

The supervisor uses the case notes to determine the therapist's skills in conceptualizing the case and also to determine how well the therapist is able to deliver the planned procedures. The supervisor may observe the differences between the therapist's plan and the therapist's performance and use this information to intervene to help the therapist improve her or his skills in planning and delivering therapy. One of the most important methods of intervening to help therapists improve their skills falls under the general name of feedback.

Feedback as a supervisory intervention. How can supervisors do a better job of helping therapists become better therapists? Providing timely, clear, and specific feedback may be the most important way supervisors help therapists improve their therapy skills (Abroms, 1977; Borders & Leddick, 1987; Garb, 1989). Failure to receive adequate feedback or receiving biased feedback may contribute to therapist's not learning from therapy experience (Garb, 1989). For example, feedback from clients to therapists may be biased by "hello" and "good-by" effects in which clients tell therapists what they think the therapist wants to hear. Therapists cannot learn what behaviors they need to correct if they are not told when they are responding in nontherapeutic ways. Supervisors must evaluate therapists' performance to provide the timely, clear, and specific corrective feedback they need to improve their treatment delivery.

Although trainees are understandably anxious about being evaluated, they still approve of supervisors who provide direct, fair, and complete feedback (Holloway & Wampold, 1983; Worthington & Roehlke, 1979). Supervisors may significantly reduce evaluation anxiety if the supervisor has built a good working relationship. A working relationship that is built on genuine respect and positive regard will allow feedback and evaluation to be accepted as an opportunity to learn rather than as cause for defensiveness and resistance (Borders & Leddick, 1987). If the supervisor develops a relationship with the therapist that may be seen as a collaborative enterprise (Stein & Lambert, 1984) designed for the therapist's good, then evaluation of the therapist's progress may become what Ryback (1974) termed "a process of self and system analysis" (p. 25). The supervisor can help the therapist to learn to analyze his or her own behavior in therapy and to analyze the complete therapy system by evaluating the impact of all the session variables; the setting, the clients, his or her history, the administrative constraints, and the therapist's interaction with the supervisor (Mead & Crane, 1978). By taking this approach, therapist and supervisor can work to help the therapist become truly self-supervising, which is one mark of the expert therapist.

Supervisory feedback may occur before, during, and after live supervision sessions, video and audio playback sessions, and case presentation sessions. Feedback may also come at regularly scheduled intervals, such as at the middle and at the end of university quarters or semesters.

When supervisors evaluate a therapist they may use an expert exemplar therapist as their template against which the treatment delivery and impact on the clients are evaluated. What do expert therapists do? They accomplish the tasks of therapy (Figure 3.1, Level 1) as efficiently and proficiently as possible. Their efficiency may be evident in their focusing on the essential tasks and accomplishing them in a timely fashion. Their proficiency may be evident in their collection of the appropriate information, their ability to formulate and test a variety of hypotheses, and their skillful use of case notes to aid their memory of the details of the case (Garb, 1989).

To provide evaluative feedback that helps therapists improve their treatment delivery, the focus should be on the presence or absence of clearly defined behaviors (Borders & Leddick, 1987). The behaviors in question should be part of the goals of supervision. Discrepancies between the therapist's performance and the treatment that might have been delivered by an exemplar therapist may be pointed out and alternative approaches discussed between the supervisor and the therapist. The two should discuss differences in perceptions of the therapist's behavior and the responses of the clients, recalling that differences are just differences, differences are not "badness." In this way the supervisor will avoid making global judgments and labeling that may be heard by the trainee as personal criticism (Borders & Leddick, 1987).

Feedback is also more easily heard and responded to if the supervisor builds on the therapist's strengths. Correct responses and improvement in treatment delivery should be acknowledged and reinforced. However, the trainee must also be challenged to try methods and techniques that they have not used before in order to develop into versatile and expert therapists.

It is recommended that the supervisor challenge rather than confront. The therapist may be challenged to discover the discrepancies between treatment attempted and treatment delivered or the therapist may be invited to attempt to examine and change ineffective therapist behaviors (Borders & Leddick, 1987). The supervisor may challenge the therapist best by keeping supervision goals in mind and then making challenges to accomplish specific behavioral steps related to the larger goals. Borders and Leddick (1987) suggest that effective challenges are: (a) tentative, such as "Could it be that . . . "; (b) include expressions of care and respect; (c) are tied to reinforcement for steps which have already been successfully accomplished; and (d) are specific and concrete behaviors and their controlling variables, rather than therapist traits.

Intervening by the supervisor for the client's welfare. The supervisor's observations and interviews with the therapist are designed to provide the supervisor with information about the therapist's skills in delivering therapy and using good clinical reasoning to make clinical decisions. The supervisor evaluates the therapist's treatment delivery skill and clinical reasoning against the responses that an expert exemplar therapist would make with the same types of clients exhibiting the same class of problems. Based upon these comparisons the supervisor then decides if the therapist's performance warrants reinforcement for being correct or, using the principle of successive approximation, for being in the right direction. If the trainee's treatment appears to be in the right direction, the supervisor delivers encouragement and reinforcement. If the therapist's response is not correct and appears to be countertherapeutic, then the supervisor performs a type of supervision triage.

To perform a supervision triage the supervisor places the therapist's erroneous treatment delivery or reciprocal acts into one of three categories: (1) those therapist behaviors that require immediate intervention—by the supervisor with the therapist—for the welfare of the clients; (2) those therapist behaviors that require supervisory intervention with the therapist but that have a low probability of doing harm to the clients unless repeated or continued over several sessions; and (3) those therapist behaviors that could use supervisory intervention to tune up some theoretical or technical point but that will not lead to any foreseeable harm to the clients. The supervisor then selects a supervisory intervention that has the best probability of changing the therapist's behavior in such a way that the therapist's behavior is more therapeutic for the clients and so that the therapist learns something about delivering therapy more expertly.

In summary, the supervisor's interventions are based upon: (1) the supervisor's observations of the therapist delivering treatment; (2) the supervisor's interviews with the therapist; (3) the supervisor's information about the therapist's preparation to do therapy which was determined in the therapist data base; and (4) the supervision goals. The interventions that are available to the supervisor are primarily manipulations of the supervisor's behavior. These manipulations consist mainly of decisions about how to conduct the supervision sessions and decisions about how to deliver feedback about the supervisor's evaluations of the therapist's performance.

The review of the supervisor's activities given above suggests that the most promising intervention approaches require the supervisor to be active at all three levels of the Task-Oriented Model. At the client level, the supervisor must observe in order to be aware of the clients' behavior and of the therapist-client interaction. At the therapist level, the supervisor must question the therapist to determine:

1. the therapist's awareness of pertinent information related to the case;
2. the therapist's use of clinical and theoretical models to evaluate what is important information and what is not;
3. the therapist's forming and testing of relevant clinical, ethical, legal, and theoretical hypotheses that are pertinent to the case;

4. the therapist's use of the information collected, the hypotheses tested, and the clinical or theoretical model to form a treatment plan; and

5. the therapist's awareness of the impact of the treatment on the clients and the clients' impact on the therapist.

At the supervisor level of the Task-Oriented Model, the supervisor must be aware of the tasks of supervision and be prepared to execute the supervision tasks to help the therapist become an expert therapist and to ensure the welfare of the clients.

Perhaps one of the most important interventions of all for the supervisor is the persistence to follow through on the supervisory interventions that have been delivered. For example, the supervisor may need to send the therapist back to collect missing data several times, following through each time to determine the therapist's progress toward the larger goal of learning to use clinical models or theory to determine what data are necessary. The supervisor may need to ask in a dozen different ways how the information gathered pertains to the clinical or theoretical model the therapist is using. The supervisor may need to ask the therapist to rewrite the notes and the treatment plan again and again until the observation sections are purged of inferences and hypotheses and the conceptualization sections clearly show the relationship of the inferences and hypotheses to the information that is known or to the information to be determined. It is in this persistent recycling, returning to previous tasks when new information requires it, frequent repetitions of tasks not completed, and continuous folding back on the three levels that the true chaotic nature of the supervision process becomes apparent.

CHAPTER 8

Determining Therapist Progress

INTRODUCTION

This chapter concludes the discussions of the tasks of the supervisor. The final supervision tasks (see Figure 2.1) are to determine the therapist's treatment delivery skills and clinical reasoning at the end of the supervision block and to compare the therapist's ability to deliver therapy now with his or her ability when the block began. The supervisor and therapist then determine if the therapist needs additional training and supervision. If further training is needed, they may begin to plan the next phase of training. If the therapist has achieved competence in a sufficient number of areas to become an expert entry level therapist, then formal training ends. However, if the therapist has not achieved competence and it appears that competence cannot be achieved in a reasonable amount of time with the resources available, then the supervisor may need to consider dismissing the trainee from the program and counseling the trainee out of therapy. As a final step, the supervisor may wish to evaluate the supervisor's gains in skills and understanding of the supervision process which may be of personal and professional value.

DETERMINING THERAPIST PROGRESS

The goal of supervision is to help therapists become expert therapists while protecting the welfare of the clients. To achieve this goal the supervisor: •

1. works with the trainee to establish the therapist's preparation to do therapy;
2. works with the trainee to establish the supervision goals;
3. observes the therapist to determine the therapist's skills in delivering therapy and the impact of the therapist's behavior on the clients;
4. interviews the therapist to determine the therapist's clinical reasoning and decision making;
5. evaluates the therapist's progress and provides interventions to help the therapist improve treatment delivery; and
6. evaluates the therapist's overall ability to do therapy and makes recommendations for further supervision or for completion of formal training.

This chapter focuses on the last supervisor task, the evaluation of the therapist's ability to do therapy and the recommendations for further supervision or for completion of formal training.

Evaluating Therapists' Progress

Formal evaluation of the therapist's competence to do therapy requires the supervisor to update the supervisor's therapist data base. Updating the therapist data base calls for a return to the procedures described in Chapter 3. The supervisor may once again ask the therapist to present a self-evaluation of his or her current skills as a therapist. The supervisor should readminister as posttests any paper and pencil instruments that were administered at the beginning of the training block. Any procedures used to assess the therapist's conceptual skills should also be readministered.

Assessment of the trainee's progress in supervision should take place on all three levels of the Task-Oriented Model—the client level, the therapist level, and the supervisor level. The supervisor's construction of the therapist data base at time two is strengthened if the assessments used in the construction of the data base include information from multiple persons and make use of multiple assessment methods. Assessment by multiple persons comes fairly naturally in supervision. The supervisor should have access to responses from the clients, the therapist, and the supervisor. Multiple methods, such as self-report ratings, ratings of other participants by the participants— for example, client ratings of the therapist, therapist ratings of the supervisor, and supervisor ratings of the therapist—and ratings by outside observers contribute to the strength of the therapist data base. The multiperson, multimethod assessment should help the supervisor to determine how each participant in the therapist's progress toward competence perceives the therapist's skill level. Because these various perspectives are known not to agree it will be necessary for the supervisor to use his or her best clinical judgment as to how best to use this information.

One way to use the multiperson, multimethod information is to compare the time one therapist data base information with the time two information. How does the therapist differ now from when he or she began supervision? The value of the written supervision plan and written supervision notes will now become apparent. Just as experienced therapists rely upon case notes and treatment plans to help their memories, so too must supervisors rely upon the written supervision plan and supervision notes, after all, the supervisor's memory is no more dependable than the therapist's.

The supervisor may now use the supervision plan to help determine if the goals for this supervision block have been met. Supervisor and therapist can attempt to determine together how near the therapist comes to matching the profile of an expert therapist in the areas stipulated by the supervision plan. If the therapist is nearing the end of her or his training, the supervisor may ask, "How well does the trainee match the profile of an expert therapist in all the areas required of an entry level therapist in the field?"

In evaluating the therapist, the supervisor must make use of all of the information that pertains to the therapist's performance. This includes the information gathered from the case files, the information gathered in the therapist interviews, and the information gathered in the supervisor's observations of the therapist's performance. The supervisor needs to determine if there is enough data to make a decision about the therapist's competence. If needed, the supervisor must make a decision about how to most efficiently gather the additional information and then proceed to do so. Once sufficient information is available, the supervisor and therapist must reach some conclusions about the therapist's progress and goals.

The supervisor and the therapist may work together to attempt to reach a conclusion as to whether or not the therapist's skills approach those of an expert therapist with these types of clients who have these specific classes of problems. If a reasonable degree of expertise has been attained, then they may decide to develop a new supervision plan to help the therapist achieve skill in delivering other classes of treatment with other types of clients.

If the therapist has had the opportunity to qualify as an expert with a representative set of problem classes needed by a competent therapist, then formal supervision is terminated. However, before termination the supervisor and therapist may work together to set some goals for the therapist to plan a personal program of continuing education. Successful supervision should prepare the therapist to maintain and add to his or her skills by the processes of self-supervision and self-education.

COUNSELING A TRAINEE OUT OF THE PROFESSION

When it comes to evaluating therapist competence, most supervisors believe they can observe a series of therapy sessions performed by a trainee and determine whether or not the therapist's performance is competent. The typical supervision process of observing and providing feedback works relatively well as long as the therapist is making progress and is gaining in skill. However, difficulties arise when the trainee begins to fall behind his or her peers.

When the trainee begins to fall behind peers, supervisors attempt to diagnose the trainee's difficulties. Once the problem has been determined, supervisors try to find educational interventions that will assist the trainee to acquire the knowledge and skills needed to become a competent therapist. Diagnosis and remediation of a trainee's difficulties in acquiring the skills related to therapeutic competence are difficult and require time.

Furthermore, as the trainee fails to gain competence ethical and legal issues begin to arise. Supervision requires the trainee to be interacting with clients because therapeutic competence cannot be acquired without clinical practice. Clinical skills must be performed by the therapist in a manner that leads to client changes for the better. If these latter conditions are not being met, the supervisor is under obligation to remove the trainee from doing therapy.

Although the goal of supervision is to help therapists-in-training to become expert therapists, there are times when this goal cannot be met. At times a trainee will not be able to deliver therapy successfully. The supervisor may try various remedial techniques while counseling with the trainee about the issues. Remedial techniques include additional practice with specified skills, additional reading, and classroom preparation, and where appropriate, personal therapy (Mead, 1988). When remedial techniques fail, the supervisor must consider counseling the trainee out of the profession. The Association for Counselor Education states the issues clearly (ACE, 1989).

Supervisors in training programs and agencies, through continual student or supervisee evaluation, must be aware of any personal or professional limitations of the students or supervisees which could impede future professional performance. Supervisors have the responsibility for recommending remedial assistance to the student or supervisee and for screening from the program or agency those persons who are unable to provide competent service. (pp. 3–4)

To assist the supervisor in carrying out this difficult gate-keeping responsibility, it is helpful for the training program staff to have established clear and specific policies to cover the issues related to trainee dismissal. Surprisingly, it is often far more difficult to dismiss a trainee than to admit one. Therefore, a carefully thought out policy for dismissal should be formulated and put in place long before it is needed.

Formulating a policy for dismissal requires the training supervisors to think more carefully about their policies for admission because there are apparently only two legitimate grounds for dismissing trainees once they have been admitted to a program. The grounds for dismissal are failure to achieve competence as a therapist and behavior that is unethical or illegal.

Before a supervisor can move to dismiss a trainee for failure to achieve therapeutic competence, it is necessary that the supervisor knows what competence is and has clearly stated his or her expectations to the trainee. This can best be done when formulating and specifying the supervision goals. The supervision goals should then be presented to the trainee in the form of a supervision plan. The trainee must have had sufficient time to learn to perform the required competencies and must have received adequate feedback about his or her progress. If these conditions have been met and the trainee is still unable to perform the treatments required, then the supervisor may recommend that the trainee withdraw from further training.

In order to dismiss a trainee for unethical behavior, it is important that trainees are told before admission what their ethical and legal responsibilities will be in therapy and in the program and what the consequences will be if they fail to comply. The ethical and legal requirements of the profession should be made known to the trainee early in the program and should be emphasized over and over again by modeling and direct instruction. This is necessary as trainees' understanding of and ability to respond to ethical issues are likely to change as they gain therapy experience (Stoltenberg & Delworth,

1987). Having a clear policy on ethical and legal expectations in place and understood by the incoming trainees makes the always difficult job of dealing with unethical or illegal behavior much easier for the supervisor.

The issues associated with dismissal for lack of competence and the issues associated with dismissal for unethical or illegal conduct are related but are sufficiently different that further discussion of the two seems warranted. Although not exhaustive, the discussion that follows should serve to alert the supervisor to some of the issues.

Dismissal for Failure to Achieve Competence

Failure to achieve the skills required to become a competent practitioner certainly is justification for removing a trainee from a therapy program. There are few therapy educators or supervisors who would disagree with that statement. The problem comes in assessing competence and determining that the trainee (a) does not now have the amount of competence expected, and (b) cannot be expected to acquire that level of competence in a reasonable amount of time and with a reasonable expenditure of both the trainee's and the program's resources. Chapters 3 through 7 have specified the tasks required of the supervisor to be prepared to make a decision about the trainee's competence. The issue to be discussed here is what to do when it is determined that the therapist does not now have the required skills and may not be able to acquire them in a timely fashion.

Once it is determined that the trainee needs remedial assistance, the supervisor must decide, with the therapist, what types of remedial efforts may be most useful. The next problem is determining if the trainee is likely to attain the necessary competence with a reasonable additional expenditure of time and effort.

It must be recognized that it takes time for the supervisor to determine that there is a problem, it takes time to diagnose the issues, and it takes time to determine and prescribe an intervention that may correct the problem. It requires even more time for remedial processes to take effect and to be translated into effective therapist performance. While all this time is passing, the trainee and the program are continuing to invest effort and other resources in the trainee's professional education. Should a decision to dismiss the trainee be reached, this investment becomes part of the issues. Therefore, the time used in establishing the trainee's problem is a critical variable.

Should a decision be reached to attempt remedial training, the time used in that training also becomes part of the problem. For example, the time required for remedial efforts may take away time that would otherwise be spent in the therapist's training and supervision. While time is being used for remedial purposes should the trainee continue in supervision? If the trainee continues in supervision while engaged in the remedial process, the supervisor and therapist must consider the consequences of that decision. Who should be responsible for the costs of remediation? If the trainee continues in the supervision and also expends time and money on remediation, does that obligate the training program in some way? Is the training program obligated to carry the trainee to completion on the basis of the trainee's expenditure of resources? If the trainee does not continue in the training program while undergoing remedial education or therapy, does the trainee get returned into the training program automatically or must the trainee reapply? The answers to these questions should be considered and be made part of the clinic's policies before it is necessary to confront a trainee with the need for remedial training.

It may seem obvious, but the level of competence we demand of a trainee undergoing remedial education should be no less than we demand of all other trainees. A trainee who delivers treatment to clients that is benign but not helpful should not be allowed to complete the course and continue on to practice any more than a therapist who makes clients worse. Remedial efforts must be aimed at developing fully competent therapists. Care must be taken that the extra expenditure of resources in the remedial training of the supervisee not become the issue when the decision must be made to retain or dismiss the trainee. When remedial education fails and it becomes apparent that the trainee does not have the skills and may not acquire them, it becomes necessary to begin to think of dismissing the trainee from the program.

Unfortunately, by the time the faculty (a) determines that the trainee is having difficulty, (b) formulates a diagnosis, (c) attempts remediation, and (d) determines that the trainee may be unable to achieve competence, the trainee may have invested a great deal of time, money, and effort attempting to reach a professional degree or certificate that he or she sees as fulfilling personal and economic goals. This investment often makes the decision to leave the program a difficult one for the trainee. The decision to attempt additional remedial training may have only compounded the problem. Therefore, the decision to undertake remedial training should be made only after careful consideration and consultation with all the training staff.

The decision to have the trainee attempt remedial education or seek therapy should be carefully thought out by the faculty, discussed with the trainee, and presented to the trainee in writing prior to entering into the remedial education process. Some issues that should be discussed and conclusions that should be reached include the following. What are the prospects for success? Who will bear the costs? If the remedial actions are successful, what will be the consequences; for example, will it take the trainee an extra year to complete the program? What will be the consequences if the remedial efforts are not successful? If the faculty allows a trainee to enter a remedial education program or suggests that a trainee undergo therapy without having these details specified, they may find that it is even more difficult to dismiss the trainee, since additional time, money, and effort have been invested by the trainee and by the program. If the arrangements described have not been made, it should not be surprising when some trainees resist dismissal.

The decision to dismiss requires that the faculty be able to provide the trainee with clear, specific, well-established criteria of competence at each step of the program. Clarity and specificity of program objectives will assist trainees and faculty in determining trainee progress or lack of progress. Obviously, a program's dismissal policy is only as good as its ability to articulate and assess its criteria for success. Lacking such criteria the program may have a great deal of difficulty dismissing a trainee should the need arise.

Dismissal for Unethical or Illegal Conduct

Unethical or illegal behavior certainly is grounds for dismissing a trainee from a therapy program. The principles that describe grounds for termination of membership as specified in the various mental health professions' codes of ethics should also apply for dismissal from therapy training programs. As suggested above, it should be made clear to trainees entering a program which code or codes apply to them and what the consequences will be for failure to comply.

Just as there are few therapy educators or supervisors who would disagree with the premise that lack of competence is grounds for dismissal, there are few educators or supervisors who would disagree with the premise that unethical and illegal behavior are grounds for dismissal. Clearly, no program would admit trainees who do not show promise to become competent therapists, and no program would admit trainees who do not appear capable of handling the responsibility of trust placed on them by clients, the public, and the profession—a trust that they assume from the moment they take the role of a therapist. At the same time, the faculty should not assume that applicants will be fully aware of all the implications of the ethical and legal responsibilities they will be assuming. Trainees should receive education very early in their training concerning the ethical and legal issues that are specific to their profession and this education should continue throughout their training. Supervisors should remain aware that they are responsible for the ethical and legal conduct of their trainees at all times. The ethical and legal responsibilities of supervisors are discussed at length in Chapter 9.

However, it seems unlikely that people who are inclined to behave unethically and illegally are going to announce their intentions in advance of admissions. Neither are they likely to announce their intentions once they are admitted to the program. In fact, they will probably make every effort to conceal any such inclinations. Therefore, the first problem for the faculty of a training program is one of discriminating ethical from unethical and legal from illegal behavior on the part of the trainee when it occurs. The second problem is deciding specifically what to do about it.

Faculty discrimination of trainee therapist's unethical or illegal behavior is largely a matter of awareness of and sensitivity to issues related to the principles set forth in the profession's ethical code. Faculty awareness and sensitivity must be coupled with close oversight of trainee therapists' conduct with clients, staff, and colleagues. In many cases a single faculty member will be unable to detect a pattern due to limited contact with the transgressing trainee. Detection of inappropriate behavior may only occur if the faculty meet collectively and regularly to review trainee progress.

Regularly established trainee reviews should begin early in the trainee's program and should continue at frequent intervals. These trainee reviews by the faculty should include observations of the trainees' strengths as well as weaknesses. Regular and frequent reviews make it more likely that faculty will detect patterns of inappropriate behavior that may need correction. Reports of these reviews should be presented in writing to each individual trainee.

When an apparent breach of ethical or legal principles has been detected, the faculty must be willing to take appropriate action. Deciding what to do about an ethical or legal breach by a trainee appears at first to be a rather simple task. If the trainee has clearly committed an offense against the ethical code or against some relevant law, then the trainee should be dismissed. However, the problem is often complicated by the word "clearly" and by our training as therapists.

Rarely are trainee therapists' behaviors clearly breaches of ethical principles. Ethical principles are generally set forth to help deal with issues that are potentially ambiguous. Decisions about such conduct are of necessity judgments by those in authority. Making those difficult judgments is the responsibility of the faculty, but clearly the process is not easy. Nor is it easy to decide exactly what to do about a breach once it has been determined that one has occurred. Part of the problem may be fostered by ambiguity between our roles as educators and supervisors and our training as therapists.

When trainees make an error in ethical conduct related to therapy, it is easy to assume that we have failed in our roles as teachers and supervisors. It is easy to assume, therefore, that we have the responsibility to provide remedial treatment. As therapists we may be inclined to believe that given proper assessment of their mistaken ethical judgments and skillful remedial interventions, trainees can improve their skills and become ethical therapists. As therapists we like to believe that therapy can help our trainees to overcome their mistakes and move them to new, more functional paths of behavior. Given enough time and effort we believe that almost any problem can be treated and the individual rehabilitated.

If personal therapy is recommended as the remedial action, then care should be taken to refer the trainee to a practitioner not involved with the training program. Referring the trainee to a therapist who is not connected with the supervisee's training program avoids the possibility of the ethical problems associated with dual relationships. The trainee's therapist should be completely separated from the decisions related to retention or dismissal of the trainee from the program.

There are several problems associated with the rehabilitation approach, especially when it comes to dealing with ethical issues. In ethical problems the time factor may be exacerbated when the trainee's behavior is manipulative and exploitive. Most often a trainee's unethical or illegal behaviors are deliberately concealed so that those who are being exploited, including the institution, will not counterattack (Skinner, 1953). The successful exploiter will not be soon detected. As a result, a great deal of time may elapse before the misconduct is detected and an attempt to apply remedial techniques is begun. While this time is passing many people may become victims. When there are many victims and the offense becomes known, many of the victims may collectively seek to counterattack the offending trainee (Skinner, 1953). In such a situation, attempts to rehabilitate the offending trainee may be seen by the victims and others as harboring the villain, as failure to protect the victims, or even as culpability.

Clearly, the decision of whether to attempt rehabilitation or to simply dismiss the trainee is a difficult one. The time factors, first to detect the problem, and second to rehabilitate, are part of the decision. Second, the needs of the victims and the onlookers must be considered. Finally, the availability of adequate resources in terms of time, money, and skilled therapists to take on the treatment must be considered. Because of these difficulties it is useful for the faculty to have decided a policy in advance that specifies what types of behaviors they have the resources to work with in rehabilitation and which types of behaviors are beyond their capacity for remedial action. This will make the decisions about dismissal or rehabilitation more a matter of policy than a decision that must be made at a time of crisis.

Regardless of which decision is reached, to rehabilitate or dismiss, a number of steps should be taken by the faculty. If a trainee is determined by the faculty to be behaving in ways that are believed to be unethical or illegal, the faculty should send the trainee a written report stating clearly and succinctly the problems detected and what is expected of the trainee to rectify them. If the trainee needs to make corrections that fall within the acceptable limits established for rehabilitation, then the trainee should be given guidance and the opportunity to make the corrections. If the corrections are not made within the time limits stipulated for the rehabilitation program, then the trainee should be counseled into other career programs. Supervisors should work with these trainees to determine their strengths and skills that may be applied in other fields. They should receive support from the supervisor as they work through their feelings and concerns. However, if the trainee will not leave voluntarily, then action should be taken to dismiss the trainee.

Once the faculty members decide to take action to dismiss a trainee, the trainee should be informed in writing. At the same time, the trainee should also be informed in writing of the proper steps to take to appeal the dismissal should the trainee choose to do so. Limits on the time to appeal should be set, allowing reasonable time for the trainee to prepare, but any appeals should be made as soon after the trainee has been notified as possible. Every effort should be made to resolve the issues quickly, so that undue amounts of trainee and supervisor time are not expended in this very difficult process.

In conclusion, when dismissing trainees from a therapy program the following steps appear necessary. First, it is important to have the criteria for success in the program be as clear as possible for both trainees and supervisors. Second, it is necessary to have established review procedures that occur early in the trainees' program and continue at regular and frequent intervals. Third, at the first hint of trouble a written record should be initiated. A written report should be sent to the trainee and copies should be kept on file. In today's litigious climate, if it isn't on paper, it isn't worth much. Fourth, it is essential to take action early so that the trainee is not allowed to expend additional resources pursuing a course of study that is proving unproductive. Fifth, the trainee requires clear procedures to follow to appeal a case and resolve grievances.

Terminating Supervision with the Trainee

At the present time, there do not appear to be any empirical studies of termination procedures for either therapy or supervision. Therefore, the discussion of termination in supervision will be confined to a theoretical discussion of termination procedures. Some scholars see termination of supervision as similar to the termination of therapy (Borders & Leddick, 1987; Stoltenberg & Delworth, 1987). The risks of comparing supervision with therapy are discussed in Chapter 2. However, since no research and little theory of termination of supervision exists, the theories of termination related to therapy will be briefly reviewed and then applied to the termination of supervision.

Ward (1984) has hypothesized that terminating therapy requires completion of three tasks on the part of the therapist: (1) summarizing progress in achieving the therapy goals, (2) reviewing procedures to maintain the changes that have been achieved, and (3) providing a closure to the therapy relationship. In addition, it may be assumed that at termination the therapist may help the clients to generalize the treatment to other similar problems and to resolve any dependency and separation issues the clients may have. At the therapist level, the therapist may use the termination session or sessions to establish follow-up procedures with the clients. Follow-up sessions may provide the clients with a therapeutic "booster" and offer the therapist feedback about the therapist's therapeutic effectiveness. As part of the termination procedures, the therapist may complete the case notes by adding a section evaluating the therapist's gains in personal and professional knowledge that resulted from treating a given case.

Similarly, in terminating supervision, supervisors may wish to: (1) summarize the progress the therapist has made during supervision; (2) discuss any further need for supervision and establish the goals for any additional supervision that is recommended; (3) establish some procedures for generalizing the processes of supervision to the therapist's program of self-supervision and continuous education; and (4) resolve any dependency and separation issues between the therapist and supervisor and bring supervision to closure. In addition, the supervisor may wish to finalize his or her supervision notes by adding a section evaluating the supervision process and the supervisor's interventions.

The procedures used in summarizing the therapist's progress, discussing the need for further supervision, and helping the trainee establish plans for continuous education and self-supervision were discussed earlier in this chapter and in previous chapters. Some comments related to the trainee's dependency and separation issues follow. Discussion of evaluation of the supervisor's supervision concludes this chapter.

Stoltenberg and Delworth (1987) suggest that as supervisors approach the tasks of terminating supervision they take into consideration that trainees at various experience levels may differ in how they respond to termination of supervision. For example, Stoltenberg and Delworth hypothesize that beginning level supervisees may be reluctant to end a supervisory relationship with a supervisor they have come to regard as a mentor. Stoltenberg and Delworth suggest that intermediate level therapists who have had a supportive supervisor may express skepticism toward a new supervisor that will make the transition between supervisors difficult. Advanced therapists are seen by Stoltenberg and Delworth (1987) as finding termination to be similar to the parting of good friends, a bittersweet experience. Supervisors who are aware of these potential reactions should be able to offer help in meeting the dependency and separation issues of their supervisees with care, concern, and respect.

Stoltenberg and Delworth (1987) also suggest that there may be gender differences that enter into the dependency and separation issues related to supervision termination. According to Stoltenberg and Delworth (1987), female supervisors and female supervisees may find saying "good-bye" at the termination of supervision more difficult than male supervisors and male trainees. This may result, according to Stoltenberg and Delworth, in female supervisors who have been supervising female supervisees not bringing the termination to a satisfactory close. For male supervisees the termination may appear too easy and the supervisor may neglect the affect associated with ending a relationship. This may result in the affect being suppressed rather than acknowledged and attended to (Stoltenberg & Delworth, 1987). Here again supervisor awareness may help as they work with their trainees at termination of supervision.

Some scholars have suggested that the final step in terminating supervision should be to present the trainee with written supervision evaluations (Kaslow, 1977; Tomm & Wright, 1982). These written evaluations should be explained to the therapist. After such explanation, the evaluations should be signed by supervisor and then signed by therapist (Kaslow, 1977). The therapist should receive a copy of the evaluations, the supervisor should keep a copy, and a copy should go in the therapist's file. If the therapist is taking his or her supervision away from the home institution, then the therapist's home institution should also receive a copy of the written evaluations.

It may appear that the supervisor's tasks are complete once the trainee has been evaluated and the supervision terminated. After the supervisor has determined that the therapist has completed the supervision goals for this time period, has achieved enough competence to be an expert entry level therapist, or is not well suited for therapy and this information has been presented to the therapist, then the supervisor should be justified in putting her or his feet up on the desk and taking a break before starting with the next trainee. Although such a response would be justified, the chances are that this approach would not lead to further improvement in the supervisor's skills in supervision. What remains is for the supervisor to take some time for some self-supervision of his or her supervision.

Evaluating the Supervisor's Progress

In the effort to evaluate the supervisor's skill in achieving the supervision goals of helping the therapist become an expert therapist and maintaining the welfare of the clients, it appears to be necessary to collect information from all three levels of the Task-Oriented Model (see Figure 2.1). To determine if the supervisor has been successful in seeing to the welfare of the clients it is necessary to have assessments and evaluations of the clients' progress in treatment. To determine if the therapist has gained in his or her expertise, it is necessary to have assessments of the therapist's clinical skills. To determine if the supervisor has been influential in changes in the therapist, it is necessary to have assessments and evaluations of the supervisor's supervisory behaviors. The discussions in Chapters 3 through 7 concern the methods used to collect information about the therapist's behavior and the impact of that behavior on the clients. The need for collection of data about the supervision process is discussed in Chapter 2 and procedures for assessment of supervision are described. Using that material to review the supervisor's progress in gaining and using supervision skills is discussed next.

By readministering any assessment instruments used at the beginning of supervision (see Chapter 2), including the supervisor's self-evaluation (see Appendix A), the supervisor may determine his or her progress in acquiring and using supervision skills. Evaluating the supervisor's progress will be aided if the supervisor has kept good supervision notes.

Supervision notes serve many of the same purposes as case notes (see Chapter 6). Supervision notes help supervisors:

1. learn which information about their supervisory behavior and the interaction of that behavior with the therapist is important to observe and record;
2. form hypotheses about the behavior of the therapist and about their interaction with the therapist;
3. conceptualize the supervision sessions better;
4. establish supervision plans; and
5. evaluate the progress and the outcomes of their supervision.

The supervision notes benefit therapists by helping the supervisor discover better ways to supervise.

As with case notes, supervision notes can also serve other purposes for the supervisor. Supervision notes, in addition to helping the supervisor to help the trainee gain skills in therapy, can help the supervisor improve his or her supervisory skills. By carefully recording observations about the therapist and supervisor interaction in supervision sessions, the supervisor may form hypotheses about better ways to do supervision, which may then be tested. The outcomes of these tests may then be organized into current models of supervision or new concepts formed as needed.

Supervision notes may also help the supervisor to communicate about the supervision with other supervisors. The supervisor may need to communicate with other supervisors about her or his supervision when, for example, an impasse is reached between the supervisor and the trainee.

Finally, supervision notes may serve as a defense for the supervisor should legal or ethical issues ever arise concerning the therapy associated with the supervision (Slovenko, 1980). Slovenko (1980) notes that one of the problems encountered in supervision is failure of the trainee to comply with supervisory directives. The supervision notes may prove useful if, for example, the supervisor directed the therapist to report a case of suspected child abuse and the therapist neglected to do so. Should the trainee's oversight later become an issue, it would be useful to have recorded in a dated set of supervision notes the supervisor's directive.

By reviewing the pre- and post-supervision assessments, the supervisor's self-evaluations, and the supervisor's supervision notes, the supervisor should be able to establish the nature and extent of the supervisor's progress during this supervision block. The supervisor may then consider setting goals for improvement in areas where skills appear deficient. In addition, the supervisor may set goals to test any new concepts that were suggested in the review of the supervision. At this point the supervisor may consider his or her work with this particular supervision block completed.

CHAPTER 9

Professional, Ethical, and Legal Issues

INTRODUCTION

In earlier chapters we have reviewed the variables used by supervisors to achieve the two primary goals in supervision, which are to help therapists to become more expert therapists and to safeguard the welfare of clients. In this chapter we review some of the more general cultural variables that influence therapists and supervisors in supervision. These cultural variables are the professional, ethical, and legal responsibilities of therapists and supervisors. In the preceding chapters the Task-Oriented Model describes supervision as occurring on three levels; the client level, the therapist level, and the supervisor level (see Figure 2.1). The professional, ethical, and legal issues also exert control on all three levels and supervisors must be aware of how the cultural variables impinge on clients, therapist, and supervisors.

Supervisors have the responsibility to assist therapists-in-training to acquire the professional attitudes and behaviors required to perform therapy. Supervisors are responsible for the ethical conduct of those whom they supervise. In addition, supervisors have a responsibility to uphold the ethical standards of the profession in their relationship with the trainee, as well as with clients, colleagues, and staff. Not only do supervisors have ethical responsibilities, but they also have legal responsibilities for the trainees' therapy training, therapy conduct, and for the outcome of the therapy performed by those they supervise. This chapter begins to acquaint you with the nature and extent of some of the ethical and legal responsibilities of supervisors.

Another class of cultural variables that have impact on therapists and supervisors are gender and ethnic variables. Gender issues are often closely tied to ethical and legal issues in that sexual involvement and harassment are forbidden in professional codes and may be tried as legal offenses in many states. Ethnic issues may be less closely tied to the ethical and legal issues of supervision, however, the ethical codes of most professional organizations state that therapists will not refuse treatment to anyone on the basis of race, sex, religion, or national origin. By implication, the same standard may be applied to supervisors accepting therapists for supervision. In addition, supervisors are responsible for helping therapists understand the implications of cultural variables, such as the ethical, legal, gender, and ethnic issues, as related to their behavior in therapy.

Supervisors are responsible for the general professional development of those whom they train. This includes responsibility for the trainees' knowledge of current clinical theory and technical skills, and the competence with which these skills are delivered to the clients. Competence in delivery requires that the therapist is capable of independent clinical reasoning and judgment about difficult ethical decisions. Therefore, supervisors are also responsible for guiding the trainees' developing professional and ethical sensibilities (ACE, 1989).

Professional and Ethical Development of Supervisees

General professional development. The problem of translating classroom and textbook learning into actual clinical performance is not well understood (Kniskern & Gurman, 1988; Lambert, 1980). However, that is exactly what supervisors are responsible for, helping therapists go from textbooks in classrooms to clients in consulting rooms. To help therapists accomplish this transition, it is necessary for supervisors to assess therapists' preparation to deliver treatment, their ability to apply clinical skills in sessions with clients, and their progress in attaining additional clinical skills (ACE, 1989). Unfortunately, assessment of therapist clinical skills is still in its infancy (Borders & Leddick, 1987; Kniskern & Gurman, 1988; Stoltenberg & Delworth, 1987). Nonetheless, the supervisor should make every effort to determine that the trainee is adequately prepared to treat these clients, with their specific diagnosis, and with the proposed treatment plan.

Professional development does not end with the last classroom assignment. Supervisors are responsible for seeing to it that therapists remain current through the use of various forms of continuous education. Supervisors should encourage therapists to employ all means available to expand their understanding of clients, clients' problems, and the processes of therapy. Effective methods for staying up to date include reading current periodicals and texts, attending and taking part in local and national professional meetings, attending workshops, and consulting with colleagues. Supervisors should encourage those whom they supervise to avail themselves of as many opportunities for continuing education as possible.

Knowledge and use of the ethical code. Supervisors should determine that their trainees are familiar with all of the principles of the ethical code or codes that pertain to their areas of professional practice. A good case book such as Huber and Baruth (1987) for family therapists and *Casebook on Ethical Principles of Psychologists* (APA, 1987) may help the therapist become aware of a range of ethical issues. Perhaps special attention should be paid to principles of the codes that point up responsibility for clients and confidentiality for those who engage in marital or family therapy, as these areas present special difficulties when one begins to do therapy with more than two members of a family in a session (AAMFT, 1988; Bray, Shepherd & Hays, 1985; Margolin, 1982; Wilcoxon & Gladding, 1985). Particular emphasis should also be placed on the principles that pertain to professional competence and integrity, as the therapist and the supervisor must work very closely together to see that the therapist is prepared to deliver appropriate treatment, but without being so cautious that the therapist never tries anything new.

As Stoltenberg and Delworth (1987) point out, trainees differ in their understanding and ability to use professional codes of ethics over the course of their training. Beginning therapists may learn and adhere by rote to codes and laws related to therapy. Ethical problems in texts such as that of Huber and Baruth (1987) are much easier to deal with than ethical dilemmas that occur in face-to-face situations with real clients. Therefore, when beginning therapists are confronted with ethical issues involving their clients, it is often necessary for supervisors to step in with direction and support (ACE, 1989).

As therapists learn to differentiate more and more subtle differences in clients' behaviors, the cases appear to take on increasing difficulty and trainees begin to see more and more potential outcomes from their ethical decisions (Stoltenberg & Delworth, 1987). This often produces anxiety that blocks effective clinical judgment and action. In addition, as therapists learn to be more perceptive and empathic with the family members, they may become too closely joined with them. This is another condition that may make it difficult for trainees to make good professional and ethical judgments and responses, especially where those decisions pit the good for one client against the good for another, as in the case of one spouse wishing to divorce and the other wishing to stay married (Stoltenberg & Delworth, 1987).

When therapists have learned to deal with ever more complex issues and cases, they come to respond with less anxiety to situations in which contradictory principles seem to relate to the issues before them. For example, ethical dilemmas arise when the therapist has received confidential information from one family member that another family member needs in order to make good decisions about their family relationships and their individual lives (Margolin, 1982; Wilcoxon & Gladding, 1985). More advanced therapists begin to handle these dilemmas in ways that are similar to expert therapists in the field (Stoltenberg & Delworth, 1987).

Ethical Issues for Supervisors

Relationships with trainees. In addition to helping trainees gain understanding in professional ethics, there are some specific ethical issues that must be addressed by supervisors. Supervisors are admonished not to exploit the unequal power relationship that exists between supervisor and supervisee. One place where exploitation appears possible is in the dual relationship of supervisors in academic settings (ACE, 1989; Bernard, 1987; Stoltenberg & Delworth, 1987). In academic settings, the supervisor often also holds a position as a member of a faculty, which means the supervisor will not only be making decisions about a student's progress as a therapist but will also be making decisions about the student's attaining an academic degree. It is important in such situations that policies regarding how information gathered in supervision sessions will be shared, under what conditions, and with whom (ACE, 1989). These policies need to be made very clear to the students in supervision along with all the expectations the supervisor has for observation and evaluation of the therapists in supervision.

Other dual relationships for supervisors with trainees that are specifically prohibited by most codes include providing therapy to supervisees* (ACE, 1989; Bernard, 1987). The point here is that supervisors should not enter into a dual role with trainees where they are both supervisor and therapist (AAMFT, 1988; ACE, 1989; Bernard, 1987). The supervisor's clinical judgments may be clouded in both directions.

---

*See Huber and Baruth (1987) Case 14, pp. 76–77 for a related case example.

The prohibition against close personal or sexual relationships between supervisor and trainee is derived from concerns about power (Brodsky, 1980). Trainees are in a situation where they are in need of supervision and may not, therefore, be free from coercion in any intimate relationship with the supervisor. In addition, if issues of sexuality enter into the supervisor-therapist relationship, it may be difficult for the therapist to discuss sexual concerns related to the trainees' clients (Brodsky, 1980). This is of major concern to the professions as many of the suits for malpractice concern sexual contact between therapists and clients (Slovenko, 1980). If the trainee cannot learn how to handle the sexual feelings that come up in therapy cases during training supervision, how well prepared will the therapist be to handle sexual feelings and responses when he or she begins to practice? Clearly then, supervisors must hold themselves away from sexual involvement with their trainees in order to be of maximum help to the therapist as the therapist works to differentiate his or her sexual and other feelings of attachment from the feelings and needs of the clients.

In supervision, issues of sexuality are not limited to sexual intimacy. Gender issues in supervision are also of concern. Sex role stereotypes appear in numerous forms. For example, there is a feeling among some clients that male therapists are superior to female therapists, a stereotype that has its parallel in supervision where female supervisors are not always well accepted by male trainees (Brodsky, 1980). However, in a recent study Worthington and Stern (1985) found that male supervisees felt they had a good relationship with their supervisors regardless of the sex of the supervisor. The same was true for male supervisors in that they felt they had a good relationship with trainees regardless of the trainees' sex. Even so supervisees thought they had a closer relationship with the same-sex supervisors and that same-sex supervisors were more of an influence on them in therapy issues. Stoltenberg and Delworth (1987) suggest that same-sex pairings in supervision may be useful for exploring issues of individual differences and professional ethics, whereas cross-sex pairings may be more helpful in discussing different views of clients and especially gender issues (Brodsky, 1980). Stoltenberg and Delworth (1987) also suggest that supervisor and therapist consider that females may tend to overidentify with the affective issues with their clients, and that male trainees may avoid affective issues by overresponding to cognitive issues. These issues may spill into the supervision process as well. Stoltenberg and Delworth (1987) provide an interesting discussion of how these gender differences in responding to affect may create difficulties related to termination of supervision. As pointed out in Chapter 8, it may be more difficult for female trainees to say "good-bye" in termination; therefore supervisors should work to see that good-byes gets said and that the relationship between the supervisor and supervisee is clearly differentiated. For male trainees the good-bye may come too easily and the affective issues may not get worked through.

Supervisors need to be aware that ethnic issues may interfere with their ability to supervise well and these issues may interfere with their trainees' ability to provide therapy to minority clients (Falicov, 1988; Gardener, 1980; Stoltenberg & Delworth, 1987). Falicov (1988) not only presents an excellent description of the issues but a very useful set of techniques for supervisors to use in helping trainees to function well with clients from cultures that differ from their own.

Competence of trainees. Of special interest to supervisors should be those sections of the ethical codes that state that students and supervisees not be permitted to hold themselves out as competent to deliver professional services "beyond their training, level of experience, and competence" (AAMFT Code, 1988; ACE, 1989).* The dilemma for supervisors is deciding when a supervisee has sufficient training and competence to try out techniques and skills that they have never tried before. The needs of the clients must be balanced against the needs of the supervisees. There appear to be four solutions to this problem— informed consent on the part of the clients, informing trainees of the competencies required for the supervision (ACE, 1989), the supervisor's careful determination that the therapist is prepared, and careful monitoring of supervisee's sessions by the supervisor.

Clients must be informed both orally and in writing that they are consenting to treatment from student therapists (ACE, 1989). Careful consideration should be given to see that all involved members of a family give informed consent to treatment including those who might not be attending sessions (Bray, Shepherd, & Hays, 1985; Kaslow, 1986; Margolin, 1982; Wilcoxon, 1986; Wilcoxon & Fenell, 1983, 1986; Wilcoxon & Gladding, 1985). Though parents can give consent for treatment of their minor children, it is important to get the children's assent to therapy as well. This respect toward the children may work to increase their cooperation in the treatment program.

---

*Huber and Baruth (1987) present an interesting case (Case 13, pp. 75–76) relative to this principle and supervision.

Before students enter supervision, they should be informed of the supervisor's theoretical model of family therapy, model of supervision, expectations for the trainee, and policies of the training agency (ACE, 1989). The therapist should also be informed of the competencies he or she will be expected to have or to acquire during the course of supervision (ACE, 1989).

Beginning therapists need careful observation of their assessment and diagnostic sessions (Spitzer et al., 1982) to prevent misdiagnoses. They also need careful monitoring of their delivery of the treatment to ensure that treatment is indeed being delivered.

Supervisors need to be aware of specific areas where beginning and less experienced therapists have difficulties. For example, misdiagnoses due to insufficient assessment and information gathering in the initial sessions is a rather common difficulty for new therapists (Slovenko, 1980; Spitzer et al., 1982). Slovenko (1980) suggests that there are three other areas where supervisees error and supervisors bear ethical and legal responsibility. Those areas are "(1) the supervisee engaging in unethical conduct with the patient which is not reported to the supervisor; (2) the supervisee not carrying out the supervisor's recommendations but saying that he did, and (3) the incomplete learning of psychotherapy techniques" (p. 462).

In some cases the supervisee may engage in unethical behavior and not even be aware that he or she has done so, which is why the behavior goes unreported. At other times the therapist may cover up the error to avoid negative responses from the supervisor. The same may be said for not following recommendations. The therapist may believe that he or she did follow instructions when indeed he or she did not. At other times the therapist may deliberately not follow the supervisor's recommendations. This latter problem seems especially likely to happen when the supervisor has not developed a relationship with the therapist that will allow the therapist to disagree with the supervisor's recommendations and directions. This condition may be exacerbated when the supervisor is male and the supervisee is female (Brodsky, 1980; Stoltenberg & Delworth, 1987). The best antidotes for all of these supervisory problems appears to be first, to establish a good working relationship between supervisor and supervisee that will allow open and candid discussion of any and all issues related to the trainees' therapy performance, and second, careful observation by the supervisor of the therapist's actual work either through direct observation through the one-way mirror or by review of the therapist's TV tapes. The minimal acceptable level of observation would seem to be review of audio tapes. Any less surveillance, especially with beginning therapists, may open the supervisor to ethical censure and even legal risk.

From the preceding discussion, it appears that supervisors may be legally responsible for the nature of the therapist's therapist-client relationships. This includes, but is not limited to, seeing that clients are informed of the nature of treatment, and the fact that treatment will be performed by a therapist-in-training (Bray, Shepherd, & Hays, 1985); seeing that clients are not exploited in any way including sexually; seeing that therapists respect the rights of clients and the clients' right to make decisions based upon an understanding of the consequences of those choices. This responsibility also means ensuring that therapy only continue as long as it is beneficial to clients, but also ensuring that clients are not abandoned or treatment ended prematurely. Supervisors are also responsible for the therapist's compliance with the laws pertaining to treatment, such as the laws pertaining to child abuse and the client's potential dangerousness to others (ACE, 1989).

Ethical issues for supervision providers. Supervisors are responsible for providing those whom they supervise with timely and adequate supervision (ACE, 1989). Numerous scholars have noted that the nature of adequate supervision has hardly been researched (Kniskern & Gurman, 1988; Haley, 1988; Lambert, 1980; Stoltenberg & Delworth, 1987). Lack of adequate theory and research related to the nature of supervision makes it difficult to determine the ethical and legal responsibilities of the supervisor in relationship to the therapist trainee (Slovenko, 1980). However, the parallel relationship of supervision to therapy has been frequently addressed (Haley, 1988; Liddle, Breunlin, & Schwartz, 1988; Slovenko, 1980). Although we have pointed out carefully that supervision is not therapy, still the parallels remain and it might be concluded that the ethical and legal issues that pertain to the relationships between therapists and clients may also apply to the relationships between supervisors and therapists. Therefore, the supervisor should consider carefully her or his responsibility to trainees as set out in the various codes (ACE, 1989). But more broadly, the supervisor might review each of the codes substituting "supervisor" for "therapists" and "trainee" for "clients" throughout. This exercise proves very informative and suggests that the supervisor has numerous implied responsibilities for supervisor-trainee relationships.

It may be helpful to look at some of the ways supervisors may be responsible for the nature of the supervisor-supervisee relationship. Supervision, like therapy, requires a well-developed working relationship. Because supervision is basically a hierarchical relationship with an uneven distribution of power, it is important for the supervisor to clarify his or her expectations with the supervisee from the start, almost as one would provide informed consent with clients (ACE, 1989; Borders & Leddick, 1987; Bray, Shepherd, & Hays, 1985; Liddle, Davidson, & Barrett, 1988; Schwartz, 1988; Stoltenberg & Delworth, 1987).

What are the ethical issues when the supervision hierarchy goes one level higher and a supervisor of the supervisor-in-training is added (Breunlin, Liddle, & Schwartz, 1988)? What are the ethical requirements for beginning supervisors? When a beginning supervisor starts to work with therapists-in-training, it seems reasonable that the trainees be informed that the supervisor is a beginner and that his or her supervision will be supervised by an experienced supervisor. Is informed consent required here? It has not been mentioned in the literature as far as I know. What are the issues of confidentiality raised here? For example, who will receive information about the supervisor-in-training's observations about the therapist and how will that information be used? Therapists entering supervision should be informed of how confidential information related to their behavior as therapists will be used (ACE, 1989; Bernard, 1987). It seems reasonable that therapists be informed in advance of the nature of the supervision they will receive, especially if it is to come from a beginning supervisor. Do they then have a right to refuse that supervision, and do they have the right to drop out at any time without prejudice to their continuance in the training program? It may be best for administrators to assume that therapists being supervised by a beginning supervisor do have the right to refuse and to terminate such supervision at any time. Programs should be planned to take these possibilities into account.

Responsibility to the welfare of therapists-in-training extends beyond informed consent. Supervisors have the responsibility not only to inform trainees about the nature of the supervision they are about to undergo but to prepare them to take full advantage of that supervision (ACE, 1989). For example, if live supervision with one-way mirrors is to be used, the supervisor is responsible to see that the therapist is adequately prepared for this experience (Liddle, Davidson, & Barrett, 1988; Schwartz, 1988). Role played sessions with practice in receiving phone-in messages and behind the screen consultations may prevent problems in actual supervised therapy sessions.

Just as it is important that therapists do not attempt to advise on problems outside of their competence neither should supervisors attempt to do supervision that is beyond their competence (ACE, 1989; Stoltenberg & Delworth, 1987). Preparation for doing supervision is just as necessary as preparation for doing therapy (ACE, 1989; Borders & Leddick, 1987). Preparation for supervision should include an understanding of the nature of therapy supervision theories and techniques, teaching skills, and consulting skills.* In addition, provision should be made for supervisors-in-training to practice in behavioral rehearsal the skills needed and then to do their initial supervision under an experienced supervisor (AAMFT, 1989). For example, new supervisors who plan to use live supervision techniques should read the appropriate literature related to the live supervision methods and should practice sending in messages of various types prior to actually carrying on supervision (Liddle, Davidson, & Barrett, 1988; Schwartz, 1988; Wright, 1986). The responsibility for adequate supervision by beginning supervisors falls upon the supervisor-in-training and the supervisor of the supervisor-in-training.

Finally, supervisors are responsible for maintaining high standards of scholarship, which includes presenting accurate information concerning therapy to their trainees (AAMFT Code, 1988; ACE, 1989). This requires that supervisors continue to expand their understanding of the field of therapy and the field of supervision by staying informed of the research and theory literature that are pertinent to both (Kniskern & Gurman, 1988).

---

*Slovenko (1980) provides, on page 463, a list of 13 additional areas where a suit may be filed if damage or injury to the client occurs. A prudent supervisor should be aware of those areas of risk.

Epilogue

The goals of therapy supervision are to help therapist trainees become expert therapists and to protect the welfare of clients. The specific domain of supervision within the overall process of therapist education and training is the application of therapy theories and techniques with actual clients in clinical settings. To oversee therapist performance with actual clients, supervisors must have skills to observe, conceptualize, and intervene at three therapy levels—the client level, the therapist-client level, and the supervisor-therapist-client level. To operate effectively at all three levels, the supervisor needs a theory of supervision.

The Task-Oriented Model of supervision provides a theory of supervision that is independent of the various theories of therapy. The model presented in this text describes the tasks required of a supervisor at all three levels of supervision. It is assumed that there are a minimum number of tasks in therapy that must be completed by clients to successfully accomplish therapy. The therapist facilitates the client tasks by completing a parallel set of tasks. The supervisor must also complete a minimal set of tasks to oversee the work of the therapist. The effective supervisor must be actively aware of the events occurring at all three levels. Being actively aware means observing, understanding and organizing what is observed, and intervening with the therapist to help the therapist become a more expert therapist.

Helping the therapist become more of an expert therapist requires interventions from the supervisor that lead the trainee to become more capable of observing affect, behavior, and cognition in her- or himself and in clients. It requires interventions from the supervisor that help the therapist to be motivated to practice therapy that is ethically and professionally sound. Helping the trainee toward becoming an expert therapist requires that the supervisor help the therapist develop a personal theory of therapy based upon the best available clinical research and theory.

The supervisor helps the therapist become an expert by helping the trainee acquire a number of technical skills:

- establishing rapport,
- interviewing to determine the problem and the variables which control both the problem behavior and the outcome behavior,
- assessing the problem by means of formal assessment techniques,
- establishing a treatment plan based upon the data established by the interviews and assessments and upon the therapist's theoretical model,
- carrying out the treatment plan,
- evaluating treatment process, progress, and outcome, and
- maintaining sensitivity to ethical, professional, and legal concerns.

The Task-Oriented Model presented in this text is designed to serve the supervisor in carrying out the complex tasks of supervision. *The model is just a beginning.* The final test of any model of supervision will be to determine if the interventions put forward by supervisors change the behavior of therapists and if the changes in therapist behaviors prove therapeutic for clients.

Appendix

PROFESSIONAL HISTORY
Preparation for Supervision

D. Eugene Mead

The information provided in this Professional History form is designed to help you and your supervisor-of-supervision to determine your preparation to begin supervision. The information will be treated as confidential between you and your supervisor-of-supervision. You may omit any items for any reason.

I. DEMOGRAPHICS

A. *Personal*
Name: _____ Date: _____

Age: _____ Sex: _____ Marital Status: _____

B. *Education*
Undergraduate: _____
_____

Graduate: _____
_____

Post-Graduate: _____
_____

C. *Current Work Setting*
_____ College/University
_____ Private Practice
_____ Clinic/Agency
_____ Free Standing Institute
_____ Other (Please describe): _____

D. *Current Professional Activities*
Please indicate percent of time spent in each of these pursuits.
_____ Administration
_____ Clinical Practice
_____ Clinical Supervision
_____ Research
_____ Student

____ Teaching
____ Other (Please describe): _____

II. PREPARATION IN THERAPY

A. *Number of Therapy Hours (approximately)*
   ____ Individual
   ____ Couple
   ____ Family
   ____ Total

B. *Your Personal Model of Therapy*
   (If you select more than one, give ranking; 1 = first, 2 = second, and so on.)
   ____ Behavioral (Jacobson, Patterson, Stuart)
   ____ Bowen/Intergenerational (Bowen, Framo, Papero)
   ____ Brief Therapy or MRI (Fisch, Watzlawick, Weakland)
   ____ Clinical Eclectic
   ____ Communication/Humanistic (Satir)
   ____ Eclectic/Integrative
   ____ Experiential (Whitaker)
   ____ Functional Family Therapy (Alexander, Haas, Parsons)
   ____ Milan (Selvini-Palazzoli, Boscolo, Cecchin, Pirrotta)
   ____ Psychodynamic/Object-Relations (Nichols, Messner, Dicks)
   ____ Social Skills Training (Guerney)
   ____ Strategic (Haley, Madanes, Mazza)
   ____ Structural (Minuchin, Colapinto)
   ____ Other (Please describe): _____

III. SELF-ASSESSMENT OF THERAPY SKILLS

	NEEDS IMPROVEMENT				EXPERT
A. *Establishing a Client Data Base*					
Observation Skills					
Self	1	2	3	4	5
Others	1	2	3	4	5
Interviewing Skills					
Nonblaming	1	2	3	4	5
Warmth/Humor	1	2	3	4	5
Relabeling	1	2	3	4	5
Self-disclosure	1	2	3	4	5
Equal Talk Time	1	2	3	4	5
Generating Between Member Conversations	1	2	3	4	5
Confrontation	1	2	3	4	5
Successful Interruptions	1	2	3	4	5

Assessment Skills
    Continuous Assessment   1 2 3 4 5
    Pre- Post-Testing   1 2 3 4 5

B. *Determining Therapy Problems and Goals*

Using theory and clinical reasoning in
    Determining Problems and Goals   1 2 3 4 5
    Determining What Data to Collect   1 2 3 4 5
    Determining the Client and Situationally Imposed
      Conditions   1 2 3 4 5

C. *Developing Treatment Plans*

Using theory and clinical reasoning in
    Developing Treatment Hypotheses   1 2 3 4 5
    Eliminating Rival Hypotheses   1 2 3 4 5
    Determining the Availability of and Appropriateness of
      Empirically Tested Treatments   1 2 3 4 5
    Determining Appropriateness of Theory Derived
      Treatments   1 2 3 4 5

D. *Delivering Treatment*

Session Structuring Skills
    Establishing Rapport With Each Family Member   1 2 3 4 5
    Reviewing Homework Assignments   1 2 3 4 5
    Setting an Agenda   1 2 3 4 5
Session Conducting Skills
    Initial Interviewing
        Individual   1 2 3 4 5
        Couple   1 2 3 4 5
        Family   1 2 3 4 5
    Using Lecture—Discussion   1 2 3 4 5
    Using Role Play   1 2 3 4 5
    Eliciting Self-exploration   1 2 3 4 5
    Meeting Resistance   1 2 3 4 5
Session Ending Skills
    Summarizing   1 2 3 4 5
    Establishing or Clarifying Homework   1 2 3 4 5
    Ending With Rapport   1 2 3 4 5

E. *Evaluating Treatment Progress*

Determining that treatment has been delivered
    Observing—Reviewing Tapes   1 2 3 4 5
    Writing Case Notes   1 2 3 4 5
Determining treatment progress
    Reviewing Case Notes   1 2 3 4 5
    Using Continuous Assessment   1 2 3 4 5

Determining treatment outcome
    Using Continuous Assessment   1 2 3 4 5
    Using Pre- Post-Testing   1 2 3 4 5

F. *Delivering Termination*

Terminating Therapy Skills
    Making Referrals   1 2 3 4 5
    Rehearsing Relapses   1 2 3 4 5
    Dealing With Separation—Dependency   1 2 3 4 5

IV. PREPARATION FOR SUPERVISION

A. *Supervision You Have Received*

(Give approximate number of hours)
____ Individual Face-to-Face
____ Group
____ Total

B. *Supervision You Have Given Others*

(Give approximate number of hours)
____ Individual Face-to-Face
____ Group
____ Total

C. *Supervision of Supervision*

(Give approximate number of hours)
____ Individual Face-to-Face
____ Group
____ Total

D. *Supervision Methods*

Please indicate the supervisory methods your supervisor(s) used with you and which you plan to use on those you supervise.

Supervision Method	Supervisor(s) Used	I plan to use
Bug-in-the-ear	____%	yes no
Case discussion with case progress notes	____%	yes no
Co-therapy	____%	yes no
Entering the room	____%	yes no
Feedback outside of the room during session	____%	yes no
Listening to a live case on audio monitor	____%	yes no
Listening to an audio tape	____%	yes no
One-way mirror	____%	yes no
Using a telephone to call into a session	____%	yes no

Viewing a video tape ____% yes no
Watching a live case on a video
monitor ____% yes no
Other (please describe)_____ ____% yes no

E. *Supervision Focus*

Please indicate the activities most frequently engaged in during supervision by your supervisor(s) and amount of emphasis you plan to give that category.

Supervision Focus	*Your Supervisors(s)*	*You Plan*
Alleviation of clients' presenting problems	____%	____%
Altering clients' patterns of reinforcement	____%	____%
Conceptualizing clients' family organization	____%	____%
Focusing on intervention techniques	____%	____%
Focusing on unconscious processes	____%	____%
Identifying and altering family structures	____%	____%
Identifying and altering nonproductive family solutions	____%	____%
Identifying and blocking maladaptive behavior sequences	____%	____%
Personal growth of family	____%	____%
Personal growth of therapist	____%	____%
Teaching clients new skills	____%	____%
Therapist's interpersonal skills	____%	____%
Other (Describe)_____	____%	____%
_____	____%	____%

V. SELF-ASSESSMENT OF SUPERVISION SKILLS

	NEEDS IMPROVEMENT	EXPERT
A. *Supervisor's Therapist Data Base*		
Establishing a Therapist Data Base		
Supervisor's Interviewing Skills		
Supporting and Accepting Therapist	1 2 3 4 5	
Nonblaming	1 2 3 4 5	
Using Warmth/Humor	1 2 3 4 5	
Self-disclosure	1 2 3 4 5	
Confrontation	1 2 3 4 5	

Supervisor's Assessment Skills
    Continuous Assessment of Therapy Skills   1 2 3 4 5
    Pre- Post-Testing of Therapy Skills   1 2 3 4 5

Determining Therapist's Preparation for Clinical Practice

    Eliciting Therapist's Preferred Theoretical Model   1 2 3 4 5
    Determining Therapist's Readiness to Learn Additional
        Theoretical Models   1 2 3 4 5
    Determining Therapist's Technical Skills
        Observation Skills   1 2 3 4 5
        Assessment Skills   1 2 3 4 5
        Clinical Reasoning Skills   1 2 3 4 5
        Case Conceptualization/Diagnosis   1 2 3 4 5
        Treatment Planning   1 2 3 4 5
        Delivering Interventions   1 2 3 4 5
        Assessing Treatment Progress and Outcome 1 2 3 4 5
        Handling Ethical and Professional Issues   1 2 3 4 5
    Determining Therapist's Awareness of Self and Others 1 2 3 4 5
    Determining Therapist's Motivation for Doing Therapy 1 2 3 4 5
    Determining Therapist's Capacity to Work
        Autonomously   1 2 3 4 5

B. *Supervision Goals*

    Determining the Supervision Goals

    Determining Therapist's Goals for Supervision   1 2 3 4 5
    Sharing Supervisor's Goals for Supervision   1 2 3 4 5
    Establishing Mutual Goals for Supervision   1 2 3 4 5

    Case Assignment

    Matching Cases to Therapists   1 2 3 4 5

C. *Supervision Plans*

    Establishing Assessment Procedures
        Continuous Measurement   1 2 3 4 5
        Pre- Post- Measurement   1 2 3 4 5

    Establishing Observation Procedures

        Using Live Supervision   1 2 3 4 5
        Using Video Tapes   1 2 3 4 5
        Using Audio Tapes   1 2 3 4 5
        Using Case Discussion   1 2 3 4 5

    Establishing Intervention Procedures

        Using Phone-in Procedures   1 2 3 4 5
        Using Knock on the Door Procedures   1 2 3 4 5
        Using Walk-in Procedures   1 2 3 4 5
        Using Planned Step-Out Procedures   1 2 3 4 5
        Using Prepared Tape Procedures   1 2 3 4 5

Presenting Supervision Plans

    Preparing Supervision Plans   1 2 3 4 5
    Presenting Supervision Plans   1 2 3 4 5

D. *Observing Therapist Behaviors*

Supervisor's Observation Skills

    Self   1 2 3 4 5
    Therapist   1 2 3 4 5
    Clients   1 2 3 4 5

Supervisor's Session Observation of
Therapist's Treatment Delivery

Session Structuring Skills
    Establishing Rapport With Each Family Member   1 2 3 4 5
    Reviewing Homework Assignments   1 2 3 4 5
    Setting an Agenda   1 2 3 4 5
Session Conducting Skills
    Initial Interviewing
    Individual   1 2 3 4 5
    Couple   1 2 3 4 5
    Family   1 2 3 4 5
Using Lecture—Discussion   1 2 3 4 5
Using Role Play   1 2 3 4 5
Eliciting Self-exploration   1 2 3 4 5
Meeting Resistance   1 2 3 4 5
Session Ending Skills
    Summarizing   1 2 3 4 5
    Establishing or Clarifying Homework   1 2 3 4 5
    Ending With Rapport   1 2 3 4 5
Using Technical Skills Appropriately
    Observing and Gathering Relevant Data   1 2 3 4 5
    Using Case Conceptualizing and Diagnostic
      Assessments   1 2 3 4 5
    Conceptualizing Relevant Hypotheses   1 2 3 4 5
    Testing Relevant Hypotheses   1 2 3 4 5
    Sharing Treatment Plan with Clients   1 2 3 4 5
    Delivering Interventions   1 2 3 4 5
    Assessing Treatment Progress and Outcome   1 2 3 4 5
    Using Self-disclosure   1 2 3 4 5
    Using Confrontation   1 2 3 4 5
    Showing Awareness of Self and Others   1 2 3 4 5
    Motivation for Doing Therapy   1 2 3 4 5
    Capacity to Work Autonomously   1 2 3 4 5
    Handling Ethical and Professional Issues   1 2 3 4 5

Supervisor's Session Observation of Treatment Impact on Clients

   Evaluating Client Resistance to Therapist Behaviors   1 2 3 4 5

   Evaluating Client Cooperation with Therapist
   Behaviors   1 2 3 4 5

E. *Supervisory Evaluations and Interventions*

  Evaluating Case Files and Assessments

   Evaluating Therapist's Case Files   1 2 3 4 5

   Evaluating Therapist's Assessments   1 2 3 4 5

  Interviewing Therapist About a Therapy Session

   Eliciting Understanding of Relevant Data   1 2 3 4 5

   Eliciting Theory/Concept Exploration   1 2 3 4 5

   Eliciting Clinical Reasoning About Hypotheses
   Formulation   1 2 3 4 5

   Eliciting Clinical Reasoning About Treatment Planning   1 2 3 4 5

   Eliciting Therapist's Perception of Treatment Delivery   1 2 3 4 5

   Eliciting Therapist's Perception of Treatment Impact on
   Clients   1 2 3 4 5

   Using Supervisor Self-disclosure   1 2 3 4 5

   Using Confrontation with the Therapist   1 2 3 4 5

F. *Determining Therapist Progress*

  Evaluating Therapist Progress Skills

   Updating Therapist Data Base   1 2 3 4 5

   Presenting Therapist's Strengths and Deficiencies   1 2 3 4 5

   Determining Therapist's Need for Further Training and
   Supervision   1 2 3 4 5

Comments:

APPENDIX REFERENCES

Borders, L. D., & Leddick, G. R. (1987). *Handbook of counseling supervision* (pp. 8–11). Alexandria, VA: Association for Counselor Education and Supervision.

Haas, L. J., Alexander, J. F., & Mas, C. H. (1988). Functional family therapy: Basic concepts and training program. In H. A. Liddle, D. C. Breunlin, & R. C. Schwartz (Eds.), *Handbook of family therapy training and supervision* (pp. 128–147). New York: Guilford Press.

Heath, A. W. (1983). The live supervision form: Structure and theory for assessment in live supervision. In B. P. Keeney (Ed.), *Diagnosis and assessment in family therapy* (pp. 143–154). Rockville, MD: Aspen.

Liddle, H. A. (1988). Systemic supervision: Conceptual overlays and pragmatic guidelines. In H. A. Liddle, D. C. Breunlin, & R. C. Schwartz (Eds.), *Handbook of family therapy and supervision* (pp. 157–158). New York: Guilford Press.

Stoltenberg, C. D., & Delworth, U. (1987). *Supervising counselors and therapists: A developmental approach* (pp. 158–160, 190–192). San Francisco: Jossey-Bass.

References

Abroms, G. M. (1977). Supervision as metatherapy. In F. W. Kaslow & associates, *Supervision, consultation, and staff training in the helping professions* (pp. 81–99). San Francisco: Jossey-Bass.

Alexander, J. F., Barton, C., Waldron, H., & Mas, C. H. (1983). Beyond the technology of family therapy: The anatomy of intervention model. In K. D. Craig & R. J. McMahon (Eds.), *Advances in clinical behavior therapy* (pp. 48–73). New York: Brunner/Mazel.

Allred, G. H., & Kersey, F. L. (1977). The AIAC, a design for systematically analyzing marriage and family counseling: A progress report. *Journal of Marriage and Family Counseling, 3*, 17–25.

American Association for Marriage and Family Therapy. (1988, August). *AAMFT Code of Ethical Principles for Marriage and Family Therapists*. Washington, D.C.: Author.

American Association for Marriage and Family Therapy. (1989, July). *The AAMFT approved supervisor designation: Standards and responsibilities*. Washington, D.C.: Author.

American Psychological Association. (1989). *Casebook on ethical principles of psychologists*. Washington, D.C.: Author.

Association for Counselor Education. (1988). *Standards for counseling supervision*. Draft paper published in Alexandria, Virginia by the author.

Association for Counselor Education. (1989, February 1). *Ethical Standards for Supervisors*. Draft paper published in Alexandria, Virginia by the author.

Baer, D. M. (1986). In application, frequency is not the only estimate of the probability of behavior units. In T. Thompson and M. D. Zeiler (Eds.), *Analysis and integration of behavioral units*. Hillsdale, NJ: Lawrence Erlbaum Associates.

Bardill, D. R., & Saunders, B. E. (1988). Marriage and family therapy and graduate social work education. In H. A. Liddle, D. C. Breunlin, & R. C. Schwartz (Eds.), *Handbook of family therapy training and supervision* (pp. 316–330). New York: Guilford Press.

Barrett-Lennard, G. T. (1962). Dimensions of therapist response as causal factors in therapeutic change. *Psychological Monographs, 76* (43, Whole No. 562).

Bartlett, W. E. (1983). A multidimensional framework for the analysis of supervision of counseling. *Counseling Psychologist, 11*, 9–17.

Berger, A., & Morrison, T. L. (1984). Clinical judgments of easy vs. difficult clients by counselor trainees. *Journal of Clinical Psychology, 40*, 1116–1122.

Berger, M. (1988). Academic psychology and family therapy training. In H. A. Liddle, D. C. Breunlin, & R. C. Schwartz (Eds.), *Handbook of family therapy training and supervision* (pp. 303–315). New York: Guilford Press.

Berger, M., & Dammann, C. (1982). Live supervision as context, treatment, and training. *Family Process, 21,* 337–344.

Bergin, A. E. (1971). The evaluation of therapeutic outcomes. In A. E. Bergin & S. L. Garfield (Eds.), *The handbook of psychotherapy and behavior change.* New York: Wiley.

Bergin, A. E., & Lambert, M. J. (1978). The evaluation of therapeutic outcomes. In S. L. Garfield & A. E. Bergin (Eds.), *Handbook of psychotherapy and behavior change: An empirical analysis* (2nd ed.). New York: Wiley.

Berkman, A. S., & Berkman, C. F. (1984). The supervision of cotherapist teams in family therapy. *Psychotherapy, 21,* 197–205.

Bernard, J. M. (1979). Supervision training: A discrimination model. *Counselor Education and Supervision, 19,* 60–68.

Bernard, J. M. (1987). Ethical and legal considerations for supervisors. In L. D. Borders and G. R. Leddick, *Handbook of counseling supervision.* Alexandria, VA: Association for Counselor Education and Supervision.

Bernstein, B. L., Hofmann, B., & Wade, P. (1986). Counselor self-supervision: Beyond traditional approaches to practicum supervision. *Michigan Journal of Counseling and Development, 17(2),* 13–17.

Bernstein, B. L., & Lecomte, C. (1979a). Self-critique technique training in a competency-based practicum. *Counselor Education and Supervision, 19,* 69–76.

Bernstein, B. L., & Lecomte, C. (1979b). Supervisory-type feedback effects: Feedback discrepancy level, trainee psychological differentiation, and immediate responses. *Journal of Counseling Psychology, 26,* 295–303.

Beutler, L. E., Crago, M., & Arizmendi, T. G. (1986). Therapist variables in psychotherapy process and outcome. In S. L. Garfield & A. E. Bergin (Eds.), *Handbook of psychotherapy and behavior change* (3rd ed., pp. 257–310). New York: Wiley.

Birchler, G. R. (1975). Live supervision and instant feedback in marriage and family therapy. *Journal of Marriage and Family Counseling, 1,* 331–342.

Blocher, D. H. (1983). Toward a cognitive developmental approach to counseling supervision. *Counseling Psychologist, 11,* 27–34.

Borders, L. D., & Leddick, G. R. (1987). *Handbook of counseling supervision.* Alexandria, VA: Association for Counselor Education and Supervision.

Bordin, E. S. (1983). A working alliance based model of supervision. *The Counseling Psychologist, 11,* 35–42.

Bootzin, R. R., & Ruggill, J. S. (1988). Training issues in behavior therapy. *Journal of Consulting and Clinical Psychology, 56,* 703–709.

Bouchard, M., Wright, J., Mathieu, M., Lalonde, F., Begeron, G., & Toupin, J. (1980). Structured learning in teaching therapists social skills training: Acquisition, maintenance, and impact on client outcome. *Journal of Consulting and Clinical Psychology, 48,* 491–502.

Brabeck, M. M., & Welfel, E. R. (1985). Counseling theory: Understanding the trend toward eclecticism from a developmental perspective. *Journal of Counseling and Development, 63,* 343–348.

Bray, J. H., Shepherd, J. N., & Hays, J. R. (1985). Legal and ethical issues in informed consent to psychotherapy. *The American Journal of Family Therapy, 13* (2), 50–60.

Breunlin, D. C., Karrer, B. M., McGuire, D. F., & Cimmarusti, R. A. (1988). Cybernetics of videotape supervision. In H. A. Liddle, D. C. Breunlin, & R. C. Schwartz (Eds.), *Handbook of family therapy training and supervision* (pp. 194–206). New York: Guilford Press.

Breunlin, D. C., Liddle, H. A., & Schwartz, R. C. (1988). Concurrent training of supervisors and therapists. In H. A. Liddle, D. C. Breunlin, & R. C. Schwartz (Eds.), *Handbook of family therapy training and supervision* (pp. 207–232). New York: Guilford Press.

Breunlin, D. C., Schwartz, R. C., Krause, F. S., & Selby, L. M. (1983). Evaluating family therapy training: The development of an instrument. *Journal of Marital and Family Therapy, 9,* 37–47.

Brock, G. W., & Sibbald, S. (1988). Supervision in AAMFT accredited programs: Supervisee perceptions and preferences. *The American Journal of Family Therapy, 16,* 256–261.

Brodsky, A. M. (1980). Sex role issues in the supervision of therapy. In A. K. Hess (Ed.), *Psychotherapy supervision: Theory, research and practice* (pp. 509–522). New York: Wiley.

Bromley, D. B. (1977). *Personality description in ordinary language.* New York: Wiley.

Burr, W. R., Mead, D. E., & Rollins, B. C. (1973). A model for the application of research findings by the educator and counselor: Research to theory to practice. *Family Coordinator, 22,* 285–290.

Butcher, E., Scofield, M. E., & Baker, S. B. (1984). Validation of a simulation for the assessment of competence in mental health counselors. *AMHCA Journal, 6,* 162–172.

Butcher, E., Scofield, M. E., & Baker, S. B. (1985). Clinical judgment in planning mental health treatment: An empirical investigation. *AMHCA Journal, 7,* 116–126.

Caust, B. L., Libow, J. A., & Raskin, P. A. (1981). Challenges and promises of training women as family systems therapists. *Family Process, 20,* 439–447.

Cherniss, C., & Egnatios, E. (1977). Styles of clinical supervision in community mental health programs. *Journal of Consulting and Clinical Psychology, 45,* 1195–1196.

Churven, P., & McKinnon, T. (1982). Family therapy training: An evaluation of a workshop. *Family Process, 21,* 345–352.

Clark, J. M., & Paivio, A. (1989). Observational and theoretical terms in psychology: A cognitive perspective on scientific language. *American Psychologist, 44,* 500–512.

Cleghorn, J., & Levin, S. (1973). Training family therapists by setting instructional objectives. *American Journal of Orthopsychiatry, 43,* 439–446.

Colapinto, J. (1988). Teaching the structural way. In H. A. Liddle, D. C. Breunlin, & R. C. Schwartz (Eds.), *Handbook of family therapy training and supervision* (pp. 17–37). New York: Guilford Press.

Combrinck-Graham, L. (1988). Family therapy training in psychiatry. In H. A.

Liddle, D. C. Breunlin, & R. C. Schwartz (Eds.), *Handbook of family therapy training and supervision* (pp. 265–277). New York: Guilford Press.

Commission on Supervision. (1989). Learning objectives for supervision course. *The Commission on Supervision Bulletin* (Vol. II, No. 1, p. 2.) Washington, D.C.: Author.

Connell, G. M. An approach to supervision of symbolic-experiential psychotherapy. *Journal of Marital and Family Therapy, 10,* 273–280.

Constantine, L. L. (1976). Designed experience: A multiple, goal-directed training program in family therapy. *Family Process, 15,* 373–387.

Constantine, J. A., Piercy, F. P., & Sprenkle, D. H. (1984). Live supervision-of-supervision in family therapy. *Journal of Marital and Family Therapy, 10,* 95–97.

Coombs, M. J., & Alty, J. (1984). Expert systems: An alternative paradigm. In M. J. Coombs (Ed.), *Developments in expert systems* (pp. 135–158). New York: Academic Press.

Cornwell, M., & Pearson, R. (1981). Cotherapy teams and one-way screen in family therapy practice and training. *Family Process, 20,* 199–209.

Coyne, J. C. (1986). Strategic marital therapy for depression. In N. S. Jacobson & A. S. Gurman (Eds.), *Clinical handbook of marital therapy* (pp. 495–512). New York: Guilford Press.

Crane, D. R. (1985). Single case experimental design in family therapy research: Limitations and considerations. *Family Process, 24,* 69–77.

Crane, D. R., Griffin, W., & Hill, R. D. (1985). Influence of therapist skills on client perceptions of marriage and family therapy outcome: Implications for supervision. *Journal of Marital and Family Therapy, 12,* 91–96.

Dodenhoff, J. T. (1981). Interpersonal attraction and direct-indirect supervisor influence as predictors of counselor trainee effectiveness. *Journal of Counseling Psychology, 28,* 47–52.

Dowling, E., & Seligman, P. (1980). Description and evaluation of a family therapy training model. *Journal of Family Therapy, 2,* 123–129.

Dustin, R. E., Engen, H. B., & Shymansky, J. A. (1982). The ICB: A tool for counselor supervision. *Counselor Education and Supervision, 22,* 70–74.

D'Zurilla, T. J., & Nezu, A. (1980). A study of the generation-of-alternatives process in social problem solving. *Cognitive Therapy and Research, 4,* 67–72.

Elliott, R., Hill, C. E., Stiles, W. B., Friedlander, M. L., Mahrer, A. R., & Margison, F. R. (1987). Primary therapist response modes: Comparison of six rating systems. *Journal of Consulting and Clinical Psychology, 55,* 218–223.

Ericson, P. M., & Rogers, L. E. (1973). New procedures for analyzing relational communication. *Family Process, 12,* 245–267.

Everett, C. A. (1980). An analysis of AAMFT supervisors: Their identities, roles, and resources. *Journal of Marital and Family Therapy, 6,* 215–226.

Falicov, C. J. (1988). Learning to think culturally. In H. A. Liddle, D. C. Breunlin, & R. C. Schwartz (Eds.), *Handbook of family training and supervision* (pp. 335–357). New York: Guilford Press.

Fenell, D. L., Hovestadt, A. J., & Harvey, S. J. (1986). A comparison of delayed feedback and live supervision models of marriage and family therapist clinical training. *Journal of Marital and Family Therapy, 12,* 181–186.

Figley, C. R., Sprenkle, D. H., & Denton, W. (1976). Training marriage and family counselors in an industrial setting. *Journal of Marriage and Family Counseling, 2,* 167–177.

Fisch, R. (1988). Training in the brief therapy model. In. H. A. Liddle, D. C. Breunlin, & R. C. Schwartz (Eds.), *Handbook of family therapy training and supervision* (pp. 78–92). New York: Guilford Press.

Fong, M. L., & Borders, L. D. (1985). Effect of sex role orientation and gender on counseling skills training. *Journal of Counseling Psychology, 32,* 104–110.

Fowler, D. R., & Longabaugh, R. (1975). The problem-oriented record. *Archives of General Psychiatry, 32,* 831–834.

Friedlander, M. L., & Heatherington, L. (1989). Analyzing relational control in family therapy interviews. *Counseling Psychology, 36,* 139–148.

Friedlander, M. L., & Phillips, S. D. (1984). Preventing anchoring errors in clinical judgment. *Journal of Consulting and Clinical Psychology, 52,* 366–371.

Friedlander, M. L., Siegel, S. M., & Brenock, K. (1989). Parallel process in counseling and supervision: A case study. *Journal of Counseling Psychology, 36,* 149–157.

Friedlander, M. L., & Stockman, S. J. (1983). Anchoring and publicity effects in clinical judgment. *Journal of Clinical Psychology, 39,* 637–643.

Friedlander, M. L., & Ward, L. G. (1984). Development and validation of the Supervisory Styles Inventory. *Journal of Counseling Psychology, 31,* 541–557.

Garb, H. N. (1989). Clinical judgment, clinical training, and professional experience. *Psychological Bulletin, 105,* 387–396.

Gardener, L. H. (1980). Racial, ethnic, and social class considerations in psychotherapy supervision. In A. K. Hess (Ed.), *Psychotherapy supervision: Theory, research and practice* (pp. 474–508). New York: Wiley.

Gilbert, T. F. (1978). *Human competence: Engineering worthy performance.* New York: McGraw-Hill.

Giller, E., & Strauss, J. (1984). Clinical research: A key to clinical training. *American Journal of Psychiatry, 14,* 1075–1077.

Gleick, J. (1987). *Chaos: Making a new science.* New York: Penguin Books.

Goodyear, R. K., Abadie, P. D., & Efros, F. (1984). Supervisory theory into practice: Differential perception of supervision by Ekstein, Ellis, Polster, and Rogers. *Journal of Counseling Psychology, 31,* 228–237.

Goodyear, R. K., & Bradley, F. O. (1983). Theories of counselor supervision: Points of convergence and divergence. *The Counseling Psychologist, 11,* 59–67.

Goodyear, R. K., & Robyak, J. E. (1982). Supervisors' theory and experience in supervisory focus. *Psychological Reports, 51,* 978.

Green, S. L., & Hansen, J. C. (1989). Ethical dilemmas faced by family therapists. *Journal of Marital and Family Therapy, 15,* 149–158.

Greenberg, L. (1980). Supervision from the perspective of the supervisee. In A. K. Hess (Ed.), *Psychotherapy supervision: Theory, research and practice* (pp. 85–91). New York: Wiley.

Guest, P. D., & Beutler, L. E. (1988). Impact of psychotherapy supervision on therapist orientation and values. *Journal of Consulting and Clinical Psychology, 56,* 653–658.

Gumper, L. L., & Sprenkle, D. H. (1981). Privileged communication in therapy: Special problems for the family and couples therapist. *Family Process, 20,* 11–23.

Gurman, A. S., & Kniskern, D. P. (1978). Deterioration in marital and family therapy: Empirical, clinical and conceptual issues. *Family Process, 17,* 3–20.

Haas, L. J., Alexander, J. F., & Mas, C. H. (1988). Functional family therapy: Basic concepts and training program. In H. A. Liddle, D. C. Breunlin, & R. C. Schwartz (Eds.), *Handbook of family therapy training and supervision* (pp. 128–148). New York: Guilford Press.

Haase, R. F., Biggs, D. A., & Strohmer, D. C. (1982). That's not my dog: A reply to Patton and Wampold. *Journal of Counseling Psychology, 29,* 611–617.

Hahlweg, K., & Markman, H. J. (1988). Effectiveness of behavioral marital therapy: Empirical status of behavioral techniques in preventing and alleviating marital distress. *Journal of Consulting and Clinical Psychology, 56,* 440–447.

Haldane, D., & McCluskey, U. (1980). Working with couples and families: Experience of training, consultation and supervision. *Journal of Family Therapy, 2,* 163–179.

Haley, J. (1976). Problems in training therapists. *Problem solving therapy* (pp. 169–194). San Francisco: Jossey-Bass.

Haley, J. (1988). Reflections on supervision. In H. A. Liddle, D. C. Breunlin, & R. C. Schwartz (Eds.), *Handbook of family therapy training and supervision* (pp. 358–367). New York: Guilford Press.

Halsing, D. W., Clancey, W. J., & Rennels, G. (1984). Strategic explanations for a diagnostic consultation system. In M. J. Coombs (Ed.), *Developments in expert systems*. New York: Academic Press.

Hansen, J. C., Pound, R., & Petro, C. (1976). Review of research on practicum supervision. *Counselor Education and Supervision, 16,* 107–116.

Harper, J. M., Hoopes, M. H., Allred, G. H., Mead, D. E., & Stahmann, R. F. (1979). The marital and family therapy skills competency checklist. Unpublished checklist, Brigham Young University, Provo, UT 84602.

Hart, G. M. (1982). *The process of clinical supervision.* Baltimore: University Park Press.

Heath, A. W. (1982). Team family therapy training: Conceptual and pragmatic considerations. *Family Process, 21,* 187–194.

Heath, A. W. (1983). The live supervision form: Structure and theory for assessment in live supervision. In B. Keeney (Ed.), *Diagnosis and assessment in family therapy* (pp. 143–154). Rockville, MD: Aspen.

Heatherington, L. (1988). Coding relational control in counseling: Criterion validity. *Journal of Counseling Psychology, 35,* 41–46.

Heatherington, L., & Friedlander, M. L. (1987). *Family relational Communication Control Coding System: Coding manual.* Unpublished typescript. Williams College, Williamstown, Massachusetts.

Heppner, P. P., & Handley, P. (1982). The relationship between supervisory behaviors and perceived supervisor expertness, attractiveness, or trustworthiness. *Counselor Education and Supervision, 22,* 37–46.

Heppner, P. P., & Roehlke, H. J. (1984). Differences among supervisees at different levels of training: Implications for a developmental model of supervision. *Journal of Consulting Psychology, 31,* 76–90.

Herz, F., & Carter, B. (1988). Born free: The life cycle of a free-standing postgraduate training institute. In H. A. Liddle, D. C. Breunlin, & R. C. Schwartz (Eds.), *Handbook of family therapy training and supervision* (pp. 249–264). New York: Guilford Press.

Hess, A. K. (1980). Training models and the nature of psychotherapy supervision. In A. K. Hess (Ed.), *Psychotherapy supervision: Theory, research and practice* (pp. 15–28). New York: Wiley.

Hill, C. E. (1978). Development of a counselor verbal response category system. *Journal of Counseling Psychology, 25,* 461–468.

Hill, C. E., & O'Grady, K. E. (1985). List of therapist intentions illustrated in a case study and with therapists with varying theoretical orientations. *Journal of Counseling Psychology, 32,* 3–22.

Hirsch, P. A., & Stone, G. L. (1982). Attitudes and behavior in counseling skill development. *Journal of Counseling Psychology, 29,* 516–522.

Hirsch, P. A., & Stone, G. L. (1983). Cognitive strategies and the client conceptualization process. *Journal of Counseling Psychology, 30,* 566–572.

Hoch, S. J. (1984). Availability and interference in predictive judgment. *Journal of Experimental Psychology: Learning, Memory, and Cognition, 10,* 649–662.

Hogan, R. A. (1964). Issues and approaches in supervision. *Psychotherapy, Theory, Research, and Practice, 1,* 139–141.

Holloway, E. L. (1982). The interactional structure of the supervision interview. *Journal of Counseling Psychology, 29,* 309–317.

Holloway, E. L. (1984). Outcome evaluation in supervision research. *The Counseling Psychologist, 12*(3), 167–174.

Holloway, E. L., & Hosford, R. E. (1983). Towards developing a prescriptive technology of counselor supervision. *The Counseling Psychologist, 11,* 73–77.

Holloway, E. L., & Wampold, B. E. (1983). Patterns of verbal behavior and judgments of satisfaction in the supervision interview. *Journal of Counseling Psychology, 30,* 227–234.

Holloway, E. L., & Wolleat, P. A. (1980). Relationship of counselor conceptual level to clinical hypothesis formation. *Journal of Counseling Psychology, 27,* 539–545.

Holloway, E. L., & Wolleat, P. A. (1981). Style differences of beginning supervisors: An interactional analysis. *Journal of Counseling Psychology, 28,* 373–376.

Huber, C. H., & Baruth, L. G. (1987). *Ethical, legal and professional issues in the practice of marriage and family therapy.* Columbus, OH: Merrill.

Hutt, C. H., Scott, J., & King, M. (1983). A phenomenological study of supervisees' positive and negative experience in supervision. *Psychotherapy: Theory, Research, and Practice, 20,* 118–123.

Isaacs, C. D., Embry, L. H., & Baer, D. M. (1982). Training family therapists: An experimental analysis. *Journal of Applied Behavior Analysis, 15,* 191–204.

Kagan, N. (1980). Influencing human interaction—Eighteen years with IPR. In A. K. Hess (Ed.), *Psychotherapy supervision: Theory, research and practice* (pp. 262–283). New York: Wiley.

Kagan, N. (1983). Classroom to client: Issues in supervision. *The Counseling Psychologist, 11,* 69–72.

Kanfer, F. H., & Goldstein, A. P. (1975). *Helping people change: A textbook of methods.* New York: Pergamon Press.

Kaslow, F. W. (1977). Future trends. In F. W. Kaslow and associates, *Supervision, consultation, and staff training in the helping professions* (pp. 302–311). San Francisco: Jossey-Bass.

Kaslow, F. W. (1986). Commentary: Individual therapy focused on marital problems. *The American Journal of Family Therapy, 14,* 264.

Keller, J. F., & Protinsky, H. (1984). A self-management model for supervision. *Journal of Marital and Family Therapy, 10,* 281–288.

Kessen, W. (1960). Research design in the study of developmental problems. In P. H. Mussen (Ed.), *Handbook of research methods in child development* (pp. 36–70). New York: John Wiley & Sons.

Kleinmutz, B. (1984). The scientific study of clinical judgment in psychology and medicine. *Clinical Psychology Review, 4,* 111–126.

Kniskern, D. P., & Gurman, A. S. (1979). Research on training in marriage and family therapy: Status, issues, and directions. *Journal of Marital and Family Therapy, 5,* 83–94.

Kniskern, D. P., & Gurman, A. S. (1988). Research. In H. A. Liddle, D. C. Breunlin, & R. C. Schwartz (Eds.), *Handbook of family therapy training and supervision* (pp. 368–378). New York: Guilford Press.

Kolodner, J. D. (1984). Towards an understanding of the role of experience in the evolution from novice to expert. In M. J. Coombs (Ed.), *Developments in expert systems* (pp. 95–116). New York: Academic Press.

Kramer, J. R., & Reitz, M. (1980). Using video playback to train family therapists. *Family Process, 19,* 145–150.

Kuna, D. J. (1975). Lecturing, reading, and modeling in counselor restatement training. *Journal of Counseling Psychology, 22,* 542–546.

Kurpius, D. J., Benjamin, D., & Morran, D. K. (1985). Effects of teaching a cognitive strategy on counselor trainee internal dialogue and clinical hypothesis formulation. *Journal of Counseling Psychology, 32,* 263–271.

Lambert, M. J. (1980). Research and the supervisory process. In A. K. Hess (Ed.), *Psychotherapy supervision: Theory, research and practice.* New York: Wiley.

Lange, A. J., & Jakubowski, P. (1976). *Responsible assertive behavior: Cognitive/behavioral procedures for trainers.* Champaign, IL: Research Press.

Lanning, W. (1986). Development of the Supervisor Emphasis Rating Form. *Counselor Education and Supervision, 25,* 191–196.

Leddick, G. R., & Bernard, J. M. (1980). The history of supervision: A critical review. *Counselor Education and Supervision, 19,* 186–196.

Liddle, H. A. (1980). On teaching a contextual or systemic therapy: Training content, goals and methods. *American Journal of Family Therapy, 8,* 58–69.

Liddle, H. A. (1988). Systemic supervision: Conceptual overlays and pragmatic guidelines. In H. A. Liddle, D. C. Breunlin, & R. C. Schwartz (Eds.), *Handbook of family therapy training and supervision* (pp. 153–171). New York: Guilford Press.

Liddle, H. A., Breunlin, D. C., & Schwartz, R. C. (1988). Family therapy training and supervision: An introduction. In H. A. Liddle, D. C. Breunlin, & R. C. Schwartz (Eds.), *Handbook of family therapy training and supervision* (pp. 3–11). New York: Guilford Press.

Liddle, H. A., Breunlin, D. C., Schwartz, R. C., & Constantine, J. A. (1984). Training family therapy supervisors: Issues of content, form and context. *Journal of Marital and Family Therapy, 10,* 139–150.

Liddle, H. A., Davidson, G. S., & Barrett, M. J. (1988). Outcomes of live supervision: Trainee perspectives. In H. A. Liddle, D. C. Breunlin, & R. C. Schwartz (Eds.), *Handbook of family therapy training and supervision* (pp. 386–389). New York: Guilford Press.

Liddle, H. A., & Halpin, R. J. (1978). Family therapy training and supervision: A comparative review. *Journal of Marriage and Family Counseling, 4,* 77–98.

Littrel, J. M., Lee-Bordin, N., & Lorenz, J. R. (1979). A developmental framework for counseling supervision. *Counselor Education and Supervision, 19,* 129–136.

Loeber, R., & Weisman, R. G. (1975). Contingencies of therapist and trainer performance: A review. *Psychology Bulletin, 82,* 660–688.

Loesch, L. C., & McDavis, R. J. (1978). A scale for assessing counseling-orientation preferences. *Counselor Education and Supervision, 17,* 262–271.

Loganbill, C., Hardy, E., & Delworth, U. (1982). Supervision: A conceptual model. *Counseling Psychologist, 10,* 3–42.

Mager, R. F. (1972). *Goal analysis.* Belmont, CA: Fearon.

Margolin, G. (1982). Ethical and legal considerations in marital and family counseling. *American Psychologist, 37,* 788–801.

Matarazzo, R. G. (1978). Research on the teaching and learning of psychotherapeutic skills. In S. L., Garfield and A. E. Bergin (Eds.), *Handbook of psychotherapy and behavior change: An empirical analysis* (2nd ed.) (pp. 941–966). New York: Wiley.

Mazza, J. (1988). Training strategic therapists: The use of indirect techniques. In H. A. Liddle, D. C. Breunlin, & R. C. Schwartz (Eds.), *Handbook of family therapy training and supervision* (pp. 93–109). New York: Guilford Press.

McKenzie, P. N., Atkinson, B. J., Quinn, W. H., & Heath, A. W. (1986). Training and supervision in marriage and family therapy: A national survey. *The American Journal of Family Therapy, 14,* 293–303.

McNeill, B. W., Stoltenberg, C. D., & Pierce, R. A. (1985). Supervisees' perceptions of their development: A test of the counselor complexity model. *Journal of Counseling Psychology, 32,* 630–633.

Mead, D. E. (1985). Computer assisted videodisc interactive simulation of a depressed client. Unpublished simulation, Family Sciences Department, Marriage and Family Therapy Program, Brigham Young University, Provo, Utah.

Mead, D. E. (1988). Dismissing a student from a marriage and family therapy program. Paper delivered at the annual meeting of the American Association for Marriage and Family Therapy, 27 October 1988, New Orleans, Louisiana.

Mead, D. E. (in press). *Clinical family therapy: A behavioral systems approach.* Unpublished typescript, Department of Family Sciences, Marriage and Family Therapy Program, Brigham Young University, Provo, Utah.

Mead, D. E., & Crane, D. R. (1978). An empirical approach to supervision and training of relationship therapists. *Journal of Marriage and Family Counseling, 4,* 67–75.

Mead, D. E., Hoopes, M. H., Allred, G. H., & Harper, J. M. (1982). The therapist professional and personal history questionnaire. Unpublished questionnaire, Brigham Young University, Provo, UT 84602.

Mead, D. E., Valentine, L., & Gay, G. (1987). *Brigham Young University family assessment and statistical recording system: A clinical multi-systems approach.* Unpublished typescript, Family Sciences Department, Marriage and Family Therapy Program, Brigham Young University, Provo, Utah.

Mendelsohn, H., & Ferber, A. (1972). Is everybody watching? In A. Ferber, H. Mendelsohn, & A. Napier (Eds.), *The book of family therapy,* (pp. 431–444). New York: Science House.

Miars, R. D., Tracey, T. J., Ray, P. B., Cornfield, J. L., & Gelso, C. J. (1983). Variation in supervision process across trainee experience levels. *Journal of Counseling Psychology, 30,* 403–412.

Michaels, L. F. (1982). The development of an anchored rating scale for evaluating psychotherapy skills. Unpublished doctoral dissertation. Colorado State University, Fort Collins, Colorado.

Montalvo, B. (1973). Aspects of live supervision. *Family Process, 12,* 343–359.

Moskowitz, S., & Rupert, P. (1983). Conflict resolution within the supervisory relationship. *Professional Psychology: Research and Practice,* 632–641.

Nelson, R. O., & Barlow, D. H. (1981). Behavioral assessment: Basic strategies and initial procedures. In D. H. Barlow (Ed.), *Behavioral assessment of adult disorders* (pp. 13–43). New York: Guilford Press.

Newsom, R. A. (1986). A methodology for determining an individual's therapeutic performance in comparison to an expert therapist and beginning therapists, using efficiency, proficiency, time, and competency variables. Unpublished doctoral dissertation, Brigham Young University, Provo, Utah.

Nichols, W. C. (1988). An integrative psychodynamic and systems approach. In H. A. Liddle, D. C. Breunlin, & R. C. Schwartz (Eds.), *Handbook of family therapy training and supervision* (pp. 110–127). New York: Guilford Press.

Norcross, J. C., & Prochaska, J. O. (1983). Clinician's theoretical orientations: Selection, utilization, and efficacy. *Professional Psychology: Research and Practice, 14,* 197–208.

Olson, U., & Pegg, P. F. (1979). Direct open supervision: A team approach. *Family Process, 18,* 463–469.

O'Hare, C., Heinrich, A. G., Kirschner, N. N., Oberstone, A. V., & Ritz, M. G. (1975). Group training in family therapy—the student's perspective. *Journal of Marriage and Family Counseling, 1,* 157–162.

O'Toole, W. M. (1979). Effects of practice and some methodological considerations in training counseling interviewing skills. *Journal of Counseling Psychology, 26,* 419–426.

Papero, D. V. (1988). Training in Bowen theory. In H. A. Liddle, D. C. Breunlin, & R. C. Schwartz (Eds.), *Handbook of family therapy training and supervision* (pp. 62–77). New York: Guilford Press.

Patterson, C. H. (1983). A client-centered approach to supervision. *The Counseling Psychologist, 11,* 21–25.

Patterson, G. R. (1985). Beyond technology: The next stage in developing an empirical base for parent training. In L. L'Abate (Ed.), *The handbook of family psychology and therapy* (Vol. II, pp. 1344–1379). Homewood, IL: Dorsey Press.

Patton, M. J., & Wampold, B. E. (1982). Troubles in modeling the counselor's model. *Journal of Counseling Psychology, 29,* 607–610.

Piercy, F. P., Laird, R. A., & Mohammed, Z. (1983). A family therapist rating scale. *Journal of Marital and Family Therapy, 9,* 49–59.

Pinsof, W. M. (1979). The family therapist behavior scale (FTBS): Development and evaluation of a coding system. *Family Process, 18,* 451–461.

Pirrotta, S., & Cecchin, G. (1988). The Milan training program. In H. A. Liddle, D. C. Breunlin, & R. C. Schwartz (Eds.), *Handbook of family therapy training and supervision* (pp. 38–61). New York: Guilford Press.

Polya, G. (1957). *How to solve it* (2nd ed.). Princeton, NJ: Princeton University Press.

Presser, N. R., & Pfost, K. S. (1985). A format for individual psychotherapy session notes. *Professional Psychology: Research and Practice, 16*(1), 11–16.

Raasoch, J., & Laqueur, H. P. (1979). Learning multiple family therapy through simulated workshops. *Family Process, 18,* 95–98.

Rabinowitz, F. E., Heppner, P. P., & Roehlke, H. J. (1985). Descriptive study of process and outcome variables of supervision over time. *Journal of Counseling Psychology, 33,* 292–300.

Ransom, D. C. (1988). Family therapists teaching in family practice settings: Issues and experiences. In H. A. Liddle, D. C. Breunlin, & R. C. Schwartz (Eds.), *Handbook of family therapy training and supervision* (pp. 290–302). New York: Guilford Press.

Reising, G. N., & Daniels, M. H. (1983). A study of Hogan's model of counselor development and supervision. *Journal of Counseling Psychology, 30,* 235–244.

Rickards, L. D. (1984). Verbal interaction and supervisor perception in counselor supervision. *Journal of Counseling Psychology, 31,* 262–265.

Rickert, V. C., & Turner, J. E. (1978). Through the looking glass: Supervision in family therapy. *Social Casework, 59,* 131–137.

Rogers, L. E. (1979). *Relational communication control manual.* Unpublished manuscript, Cleveland State University, Department of Speech Communication.

Rosenbaum, D. N. (1984). Evaluation of student performance in psychotherapy. *Journal of Clinical Psychology, 40,* 1106–1111.

Russell, R. K., Crimmings, A. M., & Lent, R. W. (1984). Counselor training and supervision: Theory and research. In S. D. Brown & R. W. Lent (Eds.), *Handbook of counseling psychology.* New York: Wiley.

Ryan, T. A. (Ed.). (1978). *Systems models for counselor supervision.* Washington, D.C.: American Personnel and Guidance Association.

Ryback, R. S. (1974). *The problem oriented record in psychiatry and mental care.* New York: Grune and Stratton.

Saba, G. W., & Liddle, H. A. (1986). Perceptions of professional needs, practice patterns and critical issues facing family therapy trainers and supervisors. *The American Journal of Family Therapy, 14,* 109–122.

Sakinofsky, I. (1979). Evaluating the competence of psychotherapists. *Canadian Journal of Psychiatry, 24,* 193–205.

Schwartz, R. C. (1988). The trainer-trainee relationship in family therapy training. In H. A. Liddle, D. C. Breunlin, & R. C. Schwartz (Eds.), *Handbook of family therapy training and supervision* (pp. 172–182). New York: Guilford Press.

Schwartz, R. C., Liddle, H. A., & Breunlin, D. C. (1988). Muddles in live supervision. In H. A. Liddle, D. C. Breunlin, & R. C. Schwartz (Eds.), *Handbook of family therapy training and supervision* (pp. 183–193). New York: Guilford Press.

Sessums, S. W. (1986). The abused spouse—Dangers for her attorney. *The American Journal of Family Therapy, 14,* 80–83.

Shaw, B. F., & Dobson, K. S. (1988). Competency judgments in the training and evaluation of psychotherapists. *Journal of Consulting and Clinical Psychology, 56,* 666–672.

Skinner, B. F. (1953). *Science and human behavior.* New York: The Free Press.

Skinner, B. F. (1957). *Verbal behavior.* New York: Appleton-Century-Crofts.

Skinner, B. F. (1989). The origins of cognitive thought. *American Psychologist, 44,* 13–18.

Slovenko, R. (1980). Legal issues in psychotherapy supervision. In A. K. Hess (Ed.), *Psychotherapy supervision: Theory, research and practice* (pp. 453–473). New York: Wiley.

Smith, D. & Kingston, P. (1980). Live supervision without a one-way screen. *Journal of Family Therapy, 2,* 379–387.

Spitzer, R. L., Skodol, A. E., Williams, J. B. W., Gibbon, M., & Kass, F. (1982). Supervising intake diagnosis. *Archives of General Psychiatry, 39,* 1299–1305.

Spooner, S. E., & Stone, S. C. (1977). Maintenance of specific counseling skills over time. *Journal of Counseling Psychology, 24,* 66–71.

Sprenkle, D. A. (1988). Training and supervision in degree-granting graduate programs in family therapy. In H. A. Liddle, D. C. Breunlin, & R. C. Schwartz (Eds.), *Handbook of family therapy training and supervision* (pp. 233–248). New York: Guilford Press.

Sprenkle, D. H., & Fisher, B. L. (1978). Family therapy conceptualization and use of "case notes." *Family Therapy, 5,* 177–183.

Stahmann, R. F., & Remell, S. A. (1983). Fee practices of AAMFT approved supervisors. *Journal of Marital and Family Therapy, 9,* 437–438.

Stein, D. M., & Lambert, M. J. (1984). On the relationship between therapist experience and psychotherapy outcome. *Clinical Psychology Review, 4,* 127–142.

Stevens, A. L., & Collins, A. (1977). The goal structure of a Socratic tutor. *Proceedings of the Association for Computing Machinery,* Annual Conference (pp. 256–263).

Stier, S., & Goldenberg, I. (1975). Training issues in family therapy. *Journal of Marriage and Family Counseling, 1,* 63–68.

Stiles, W. B., & Snow, J. S. (1984). Counseling session impact as viewed by novice counselors and their clients. *Journal of Counseling Psychology, 31,* 3 –12.

Stoltenberg, C. D. (1981). Approaching supervision from a developmental perspective: The counselor complexity model. *Journal of Counseling Psychology, 28,* 59–65.

Stoltenberg, C. D., & Delworth, U. (1987). *Supervising counselors and therapists: A developmental approach.* San Francisco: Jossey-Bass.

Stoltenberg, C. D., Pierce, R. A., & McNeill, B. W. (1987). Effects of experience on counselor needs. *The Clinical Supervisor, 5,* 23–32.

Stone, G. L. (1980). Effects of experience on supervisor planning. *Journal of Counseling Psychology, 27,* 84–88.

Stone, G. L., & Vance, A. (1976). Instructions, modeling, and rehearsal: Implications for training. *Journal of Counseling Psychology, 23,* 272–279.

Storm, C. L., & Heath, A. W. (1985). Models of supervision: Using therapy as a guide. *The Clinical Supervisor, 3,* 87–96.

Street, E., & Treacher, A. (1980). Microtraining and family therapy skills—towards a possible synthesis. *Journal of Family Therapy, 2,* 243–257.

Strohmer, D. C., Biggs, D. A., Haase, R. F., & Keller, K. E. (1983). Hypothesis formation and testing in clinical judgment. *Journal of Counseling Psychology, 30,* 607–610.

Strohmer, D. C., Haase, R. F., Biggs, D. A., & Keller, K. E. (1982). Process models of counselor judgment. *Journal of Counseling Psychology, 29,* 597–606.

Strohmer, D. C., & Newman, L. J. (1983). Counselor hypothesis-testing strategies. *Journal of Counseling Psychology, 30,* 557–565.

Strong, S. R. (1987). Interpersonal influence theory as a common language for psychotherapy. *Journal of Integrative and Eclectic Psychotherapy, 6,* 173–184.

Strong, S. R., & Hills, H. I. (1986). *Interpersonal communication rating scale.* Unpublished manuscript, Virginia Commonwealth University, Department of Psychology, Richmond, Virginia.

Styczynski, L. E. (1980). The transition from supervisee to supervisor. In A. K. Hess (Ed.), *Psychotherapy supervision: Theory, research and practice* (pp. 29–40). New York: Wiley.

Thelen, M. H., Fry, R. A., Fehrenbach, P. A., & Frautschi, N. M. (1979). Therapeutic videotape and film modeling: A review. *Psychological Bulletin, 86,* 701–720.

Thompson, A. J. M., & Blocher, D. H. (1979). Co-counseling supervision in microcounseling. *Journal of Counseling Psychology, 26,* 413–418.

Thoresen, C. E. (1969). The systems approach and counselor education: Basic features and implications. *Counselor Education and Supervision, 9,* 3–17.

Tomm, K. M., & Sanders, G. L. (1983). Family assessment in a problem oriented record. In J. C. Hansen & B. P. Keeney (Eds.), *Diagnosis and assessment in family therapy* (pp.103–122). Rockville, MD: Aspen Systems.

Tomm, K. M., & Wright, L. M. (1979). Training in family therapy: Perceptual, conceptual, and executive skills. *Family Process, 18,* 227–250.

Tomm, K. M., & Wright, L. M. (1982). Multilevel training and supervision in an outpatient service programme. In R. Whiffen & J. Byng-Hall (Eds.), *Family therapy supervision: Recent developments in practice* (pp. 211–227). London: Academic Press.

Truax, C. B., & Carkhuff, R. R. (1967). *Toward effective counseling and psychotherapy: Training and practice.* Chicago: Aldine.

Tucker, B. Z., Hart, G., & Liddle, H. A. (1976). Supervision in family therapy: A developmental perspective. *Journal of Marriage and Family Counseling, 2,* 269–276.

Valentine, L. (1986). Construct validity of an interactive computer-assisted videodisc simulation for cognitive therapy of depression. Unpublished master's thesis. Brigham Young University, Provo, Utah.

Walz, G. R., & Johnson, J. A. (1963). Counselors look at themselves on video-tape. *Journal of Counseling Psychology, 10,* 232–236.

Ward, D. E., (1984). Termination of individual counseling: Concepts and strategies. *Journal of Counseling and Development, 63,* 21–25.

Ward, L. G., Friedlander, M. L., Schoen, L. G., & Klein, J. G. (1985). Strategic self-presentation in supervision. *Journal of Counseling Psychology, 32,* 111–118.

Watzlawick, P. (1966). A structured family interview. *Family Process, 5,* 256–271.

Webster's Ninth New Collegiate Dictionary. (1984). Springfield, MA: Merriam-Webster.

Wendorf, D. J. (1984). A model for training practicing professionals in family therapy. *Journal of Marital and Family Therapy, 10,* 31–41.

Wetchler, J. L. (1989). Supervisors' and supervisees' perceptions of the effectiveness of family therapy supervisor interpersonal skills. *The American Journal of Family Therapy, 17,* 244–256.

Wetchler, J. L., Piercy, F. P., & Sprenkle, D. H. (1989). Supervisors' and supervisees' perceptions of the effectiveness of family therapy supervisory techniques. *The American Journal of Family Therapy, 17,* 35–47.

Wiffen, R. (1982). The use of videotape in supervision. In R. Wiffen & J. Byng-Hall (Eds.). *Family therapy supervision: Recent developments in practice.* London: Academic Press.

Wiffen, R., & Byng-Hall, J. (1982). (Eds.), *Family therapy supervision: Recent developments in practice.* London: Academic Press.

Wilcoxon, S. A. (1986). One-spouse marital therapy: Is informed consent necessary? *The American Journal of Family Therapy, 14,* 265–270.

Wilcoxon, S. A., & Fennell, D. L. (1983). Engaging the non-attending spouse in marital therapy through the use of therapist-initiated written communication. *Journal of Marital and Family Therapy, 9,* 199–203.

Wilcoxon, S. A., & Fennell, D. L. (1986). Linear and paradoxical letters to the non-attending spouse: A comparison of engagement rates. *Journal of Marital and Family Therapy, 12,* 191–193.

Wilcoxon, S. A., & Gladding, S. T. (1985). Engagement and termination in marital and family therapy: Special ethical issues. *The American Journal of Family Therapy, 13* (4), 65–71.

Wiley, M. O. (1982). *Developmental counseling supervision: Person-environment congruency, satisfaction, and learning.* Paper presented at the annual meeting of the American Psychological Association, Washington, D.C.

Wilson, L. (1981). Thoughts on Tarasoff. *Clinical Psychologist, 34,* 37.

Wolberg, L. R. (1954). *The technique of psychotherapy.* New York: Grune and Stratton.

Worthington, E. L., Jr., (1984a). Empirical investigation of supervision of counselors as they gain experience. *Journal of Counseling Psychology, 31,* 63–75.

Worthington, E. L., Jr., (1984b). Supervisors as empathic observers of counselor behavior. *Professional Psychology: Research and Practice, 15,* 457–461.

Worthington, E. L., Jr., (1984c). Use of trait labels in counseling supervision by experienced and inexperienced supervisors. *Professional Psychology: Research and Practice, 15,* 457–461.

Worthington, E. L., Jr., & Roehlke, H. J. (1979). Effective supervision as perceived by beginning counselors-in-training. *Journal of Counseling Psychology, 26,* 64–73.

Worthington, E. L., Jr., & Stern, A. (1985). Effects of supervisor and supervisee degree level and gender on the supervisory relationship. *Journal of Counseling Psychology, 32,* 252–262.

Wright, J., & Mathieu, M., McDonough, C. (1981). An evaluation of three approaches to the teaching of a behavioral therapy. *Journal of Clinical Psychology, 37,* 326–335.

Wright, L. M. (1986). An analysis of live supervision "phone-ins" in family therapy. *Journal of Marital and Family Therapy, 12,* 187–190.

Wright, L. M., & Coppersmith, E. I. (in press). Supervision of supervision: How to be "meta" to a metaposition.

Wright, L. M., & Leahey, M. (1988). Nursing and family therapy training. In H. A. Liddle, D. C. Breunlin, & R. C. Schwartz (Eds.), *Handbook of family therapy training and supervision* (pp. 278–289). New York: Guilford Press.

Yogev, S., & Pion, G. M. (1984). Do supervisors modify psychotherapy supervision according to supervisees' levels of experience? *Psychotherapy, 21,* 206–208.

Name Index

Subject Index

Administrative constraints, 14, 40, 56, 74, 97, 105, 112; manipulation of, by supervisor, 106. *See also* Supervision variables

Advanced therapist experience level, 5–6, 9–10, 15, 24, 48, 55–56, 107, 128, 135; defined 7–8, observation of, 71–72. *See also* Experience levels of therapists; Therapist experience levels

Affective responses of therapists, 7, 9, 14, 61, 65, 75, 77, 86, 88, 93–94, 101, 128, 136; Assessment of, 49; Supervision goals and, 53–54. *See also* Anxiety

Anxiety, 48, 104, 112, 134; Assessment of, 32; Causes of, 9, 134–135. *See also* Affective responses

Assessment: of clients, 76, 97; live supervision and 70; of supervisor, 30–32, 76, 97, 102, 129–131; of supervisor interventions, 32, 49; of supervisor's professional history, 30–31, 145–153; of therapist, 32, 46, 49, 76, 118; of therapist affect 32, 49; of therapist conceptualization and clinical reasoning, 41–42, 99; of therapist motivation, 47–49; of therapist progress, 96–97, 117–118; selecting procedures for, 75–77; of therapist skills 40–41, 82, 97; use of exemplar therapist and, 100–102

Audio tapes, 19, 37, 71

Barrett-Lennard Relationship Inventory, 40, 41

Beginning therapist experience level, 14, 55–56, 98, 128, 134, 138; defined, 7–8; observation of, 70–73. *See also* Experience levels of therapists; Therapist experience levels

Behavioral theory: supervision and, 16n, 16–71, 23; Task-Oriented Model and, 24

Blumberg's Interactional Analysis, 32

Brief therapy, 17

"Burn-out": of therapist, 48

Case assignment, 37–38, 77

Case consultation, 20

Case notes, 69, 72, 74, 109–110, 112; format for Figure 6.1, 90–92; preparation of, 37, 88–89, 93–95; evaluation of, by supervisor, 88–89, 109–111; therapist's use of, 112

Client-centered model, 17, 23

Clients, 84, 94; assigning to therapist, 38; client level of Task-Oriented model, 21, 23–25, 97–98; consent to treatment, 137; evaluation of, 26; as nonstandard stimuli, 83–84; as standard stimuli, 82; general model of, 23–24; home work assigned to, 94–95; simulation of, 83; tasks of, 24, 85. *See also* Case assignment; Task-Oriented Model, levels

Client welfare, 5, 17, 73; intervention for, by supervisor, 97, 113–114; supervisor's responsibility for, 5, 101

Clinical Assessment Questionnaire, 47

Clinical judgment, 74. *See also* Clinical reasoning

Clinical model, 18–19

Clinical practice, 38–39; assessing therapist readiness for, 39; conceptual skills for, 41–42

Clinical reasoning: client welfare and, 101, 108–109; evaluating therapist's use of, 26, 43–45, 85–88, 98, 101–102; evaluation of therapist performance, 43–45, 98, 118; interviews to determine therapist's use of, 43–45, 80, 85–88, 99; supervisor's 29–30; therapist's anxiety and, 134; timeliness of interviews to determine, 75; use of the Task-Oriented Model and, 85

Clinical setting, 13–14. *See also* Consulting room

Colleague role: in supervision, 10

Communication, 36, 52

Competence: failure of therapist to achieve,